Breaking Free
from the Victim Trap:

Reclaiming Your Personal Power

Diane Zimberoff, M.A.

WELLNESS PRESS   ISSAQUAH, WA, USA

Published by:

Wellness Press
The Wellness Institute
3716 274th Ave SE
Issaquah, WA 98029 USA
425-391-9716
800-326-4418

Library of Congress Catalog Card Number: 89-050730

ISBN 0-9622728-0-9

Table of Contents

PART 2: Treatment: Turning the Victim Triangle into
A Circle of Power through Personal Transformation

Chapter 11   **How Hypnosis Works in Treatment**   101
             Age Regressions

Chapter 12   **Treatment of Victim Patterns**   105
             Changing Helplessness to Assertiveness ❖
             Moving from Self-pity to Self-esteem ❖
             Turning from Blame to Personal Power ❖
             Changing Guilt to Forgiveness ❖
             Approval from Others to Approval from Within ❖
             The Personal Transformation Process ❖
             Defining Healthy Love & Codependency   112

Chapter 13   **Changing the Pattern of Rescuing**   113
             Releasing Responsibility for Others ❖
             Knowing That Your Needs Are Important ❖
             Taking Responsibility to Have Your Needs Met ❖
             Eliminating Guilt Trips ❖ Releasing the Anger ❖
             Healthy Release of Anger ❖ Anger and Addictions ❖
             Releasing Responsibility for Others/
             Becoming Responsible for Oneself ❖
             Giving Others Back their Power/Claiming Your Power ❖
             Illustration: Codependency to Inter-Dependency   120-121

Chapter 14   **Healing the Persecutor Personality**   123
             Releasing Blame ❖ Extinguishing Addictions ❖
             Clear Boundaries ❖ Healing Shame ❖
             Eliminating Persecutor Patterns   127

Chapter 15   **Healing the Victim Personality**   129
             Reuniting With the Child Within ❖
             Unconditional Love ❖
             How Were Feelings Dealt with in Your Family? 141

Chapter 16   **The Personal Transformation Intensive**   147
             Breathwork and Rebirthing ❖ Energetic Psychodrama ❖
             The Master Mind Process ❖ Meditation
             Illustration: Personal Transformation Chart   159

Endnotes   167
References   173
Index   177

FOREWORD to the First Edition (1989)

The Victim Game is a family game which is taught to children in three ways.

The first is by direct example, since one or more of the parents is usually a victim in families where this game is played.

Second, the child is programmed by the parent to be a victim.

Third, the victim behavior is reinforced by the parent until it becomes a permanent part of the child's identity.

The child then goes through life having one victim experience after another and each experience reinforces this person's victim position.

This victim programming is the basis of most of today's individual, as well as family and corporate, problems. The game is insidious, especially because it is taught in the family. If there are four children in the family, these four children will all grow up, possibly marry other victims and then raise another four families of victims. So the numbers keep multiplying.

The Victim Game can be stopped and changed, but it takes (1) desire to change, (2) conscious awareness, and (3) intensive therapy to change the subconscious programming.

This book is intended to identify the victim personality, describe how the victim is molded, help the reader to see if this applies to him/her and explain some of the treatment techniques that have been found effective. Case histories assist the reader in recognizing this syndrome if it does exist in his/her life.

FOREWORD to the Fourth Edition (2004)

This book is now in its fifteenth year, with 21,000 copies sold. Over these fifteen years, I have received thousands of letters, phone calls, emails and personal responses from people telling me how much this information has changed their lives. Most people immediately recognize their own families as well as their places of employment such as agencies, school systems and corporations. People take their victim patterns with them wherever they go.

We have taught our Heart-Centered Hypnotherapy training and our advanced Internship programs to thousands of professionals around the world. We have trained those professionals to lead the Personal Transformation Intensive (PTI) for their clients and people in their communities. One thing we have discovered is that healing the victim consciousness is relevant to a vast majority of people in our society. Regardless of whether we are working with highly trained professionals or "just plain folks," they all have aspects of victim, rescuer and persecutor in their personalities. The concept is universal and continues to be relevant even after the fifteen years this book has been in print. There is more demand for the book now than ever, and we continue to publish it with great joy and hope that it will bring healing to you and your family as it has to so many others.

We have revised the book significantly, adding two new chapters to more completely explain the current concepts we work with and the tools and techniques that we use to break through the victim triangle. These tools have proven very effective over the years, and we hope that you will have a chance to experience them in person.

PART I

Identifying the Victim Triangle,
the Dysfunctional Family and Codependency

Chapter 1
The Dysfunctional Family

You can tell what is happening in your consciousness by the people that
you attract into your life. If you have a lot of victims in your life, you
can be sure that you are a rescuer.

Every dysfunctional family includes a special needs person, the victim,
who in many cases is an alcoholic, sex addict or drug addict. This person
could also be someone in the family who is mentally retarded, mentally ill,
or has some particular problem that draws a lot of attention. It could be a
grandmother who is sick and old and has come to live with the family.
Basically, it can be anyone or any set of circumstances that require special
attention. In this family, this special needs person takes up a lot of time
and energy so that the others' needs simply don't get met.

Children growing up in dysfunctional families are so concerned with
taking care of the sick person, the alcoholic, or the addict, that they begin
to put themselves second or third, assuming that their own needs will not
be met. In fact, these children grow up not even knowing what their needs
are because they are so tuned into taking care of the family and the other
person. This is how they become rescuers.

Moreover, this dysfunctional family is walking around on eggshells,
with everyone being super sensitive not to upset the victim. For example,
the special needs or victim person might be a father with a nasty temper.
Set him off and he will go on a rampage and everybody is going to be in
trouble. The same is true with an alcoholic; they don't want to agitate him
or he might go out and drink. And there is a great deal of caution with a
mentally ill person, because he might have a nervous breakdown or be
shipped off to the hospital.

Another common phenomenon in the dysfunctional family is that the
family members become addicted to chaos and drama. The special needs
person may go off and get drunk or lose his temper, so the family must
learn how to deal with these crisis situations. If you have been raised in
this type of dysfunctional family, you may find that you are drawn into
relationships in which your needs are not met. You may also attract a
relationship in which somehow there is always a crisis brewing and you
feel responsible to fix everything. People have a tendency to re-create the
patterns they experienced early in their lives. An addiction to chaos is one

3

of those familiar patterns. When things are mellow and calm, you feel bored and irrelevant. It's like waiting for the other shoe to drop. Any minute now this wonderful space is going to be broken by something terrible happening. So you're always walking around with anxiety, especially when things are good. People from dysfunctional families can't even enjoy times of peace and tranquillity because they have a knot in their stomachs from anticipating the worst.

Another result of growing up in a dysfunctional family is the fear of intimacy. Most of these people have no idea what intimacy is. In fact, many times intimacy to them means fighting. The only way they really have an intense one-on-one involvement is when there is a fight. Otherwise the special needs person is off getting drunk or having a nervous breakdown or creating some other victim situation. Everybody else is cleaning up the mess (rescuing), and nobody has any real closeness or true intimacy. So these individuals grow up attracting other people into their lives who themselves don't know how to experience intimacy except through fighting and chaos. Intimacy begins to feel like pain, something to avoid at all cost.

Dysfunctional families also have about them a cloudy sense of unpredictability; you never know what is going to happen next. Accordingly, the child is afraid to bring her friends home because dad might be drunk on the floor, or might come home and lose his temper and embarrass her. Or she could come home and find that her mother is so depressed that she has her head in the oven, inhaling gas to try to kill herself. This unpredictability causes great anxiety and feelings of insecurity for a child.

In the dysfunctional family there are a lot of rules. The problem with these rules is that they are often unspoken. The most common unspoken rule in the dysfunctional family is: "Don't speak." Children are to be seen and not heard. "Be quiet. Go to your room. Don't talk back." Those are the typical messages in this family. So the child gets the message early and often that it is not okay to be himself, to speak his truth. Another rule is: "Don't trust! Don't trust outsiders, don't trust the neighbors, and especially don't trust your teacher. We don't hang our dirty laundry in public." This type of brainwashing gives the message that somehow the people out there are the enemy, that we have to be careful of other people. This is the kind of paranoia that permeates dysfunctional families.

The most devastating consequence of this conditioning is that these children learn not to trust themselves. They learn not to trust their own intuition because whenever they say something about how they feel, they are immediately told, "Shut up," "You're stupid," or "You're being disrespectful." So they can't even trust their own perceptions about what is happening around them.

Another common occurrence in dysfunctional families is that there is no resolution of conflict. At night the parents are fighting and maybe even hitting each other. The next morning everything is "fine" and they are pretending nothing happened. When the child asks about it, they are told everything is fine. Parents go to bed fighting and wake up smiling and nothing is ever talked about. So the child receives confused messages; they learn not to trust their own perceptions of reality.

The child is bombarded with messages that say: "Don't trust other people. Don't speak. Don't feel. Don't express your feelings. Just be good." Being good means being a little "robot" walking around and pretending, with a smile on your face. It takes a lot of energy for children to pretend, to put on an act, and to keep all their feelings inside.

Children of dysfunctional families become very confused, and this is the beginning of their addictions. It is really the source of compulsive behavior because in order to keep their feelings suppressed, children observe how the adults keep their own feelings suppressed. Kids notice everything. They watch the parents using alcohol or drugs or tobacco or stuffing themselves with food. Stuffing feelings down with food is one of the most common compulsive behaviors. Perhaps a child at that point may grab a handful of cookies and go in their room and eat them when they feel sad or upset or scared. So they begin to become numb and dissociated from their emotions. This is the basis of addictive behavior: disconnecting from your feelings and becoming numb.

Another family rule is, "Don't be yourself." In the dysfunctional family there is a private self and a public self (see illustration on page 11). The public self is devoted to the images, the roles, and the facade of a happy smiling face. This is what the family wants the child to show to the outside world. The private self has all the feelings, the fears, the insecurities, and the deep inner secrets. These two selves are usually worlds apart. In order to keep the private self hidden and the facade intact, it takes more and more drugs or cigarettes or alcohol or sex or food. It takes a lot of addictive behavior to keep pushing down the feelings, fears and emotions of a lifetime. This is the source of addictive behavior.

One of the things that makes this private self so private is shame, because all dysfunctional families are shame-based. The parents say; "Shame on you. You should be ashamed of yourself. Look what you did. You're embarrassing me in front of all my friends. What will the

5

neighbors think?" These messages are designed to control and manipulate the child, and the child begins to feel ashamed of who he is, of the very essence of his *being*. The child takes on the shame of the "family secret," the shame that Dad is an alcoholic, or Mom has a mental illness, or that the sibling is retarded, or the sister was molested by the uncle. Whatever the shame is, the child identifies with it as if he had done something wrong. The public self and the private self grow further apart as the child is hiding the private self, which includes the shame, and tries to do his part to save the family image. The child really exists to keep up the roles and the image of the family.

The Victim Triangle

I'm now going to introduce you to the *victim triangle*[1] (see illustration on page 10). The victim triangle is the basis for codependent dysfunctional families and also for addictions. At the top of this triangle is the victim. The victim is a person who feels helpless and sorry for himself. He blames other people for his problems. "If it weren't for you I could be happy. If it weren't for the government I could be rich." By continuing to blame everyone and everything in sight, that person is giving away his power. This is what keeps the victim feeling helpless and powerless. The victim triangle is about a lack of personal power.

In the bottom left position of the diagram is what we call the *rescuer*. Within the rescuer is also a victim consciousness. The rescuer is the person who takes care of everybody else, the child who grew up in that dysfunctional family who thinks that it is her responsibility to solve the family's problems or to take care of her alcoholic father.

I have worked with people who, through hypnosis, can relive being five-year-olds washing clothes, doing dishes, and making lunches for the other kids because their parents were incapable or unavailable to take care of the children. Five years old and they are taking care of the family! This is exactly how a rescuer develops. Underneath their "helpful" exterior, rescuers feel like victims. What they do in order to stop feeling like a victim is to try to rescue another victim. They find someone who is just a little bit weaker than they are, a little bit more needy. This is where codependency emerges. Each person/role becomes dependent on the other to satisfy their emotional needs. The rescuer is dependent on the victim to remain helpless. The victim is dependent on the rescuer to take care of him. These dependencies may not be observable to the untrained eye. On the surface these people may look happy and fulfilled. They come from

6

diverse socio-economic levels. They know how to hide the victim consciousness because they come from a dysfunctional family where they were taught to create a "successful-looking" public self.

The victim and the rescuer continue to become more and more codependent on each other. The rescuer keeps trying to "fix" the victim. This causes the victim to feel even more helpless, and consequently quite resentful. This resentment, in turn, brings about a reversal and the victim becomes the persecutor. Underneath, however, the persecutor continues to feel like a victim.

Persecution can take many forms. People can persecute with abuse, either physical, emotional, or sexual. They may be persecuting by withdrawal of love, sexual gratification, or financial security. An example is the father/husband who walks into the house, sits down and retreats behind his newspaper. Someone asks, "Well, what's wrong?" and the reply is, "Nothing." He will not talk about his feelings, even though everyone in the house can sense his anger. This is a means of persecution: covert anger or passive aggression. Another means of persecution is laying guilt trips on others to control and manipulate them. There are many different ways to persecute, some more subtle than others.

The persecutor persecutes the rescuer. Then the rescuer feels like a victim. The persecutor feels pity for the victim, and moves to rescue her. The victim resents the feeling of helplessness in being rescued, and moves to persecute the rescuer. They are constantly going around in this vicious circle (triangle), moving from one position to the next.

This is where the individual boundaries become really unclear. Unclear personal boundaries are characteristic of dysfunctional families; people don't know who they are, and consequently they get their identities confused with each other. These boundaries get diffuse because the family members are jumping back and forth from one position in the triangle to another. In some families they just jump back and forth between victim and rescuer. Other families oscillate between victim and persecutor, fighting constantly.

It is common in these families for the children to jump in on the rescuer position, trying to make things better. Many times you can hear the victim positions in the children, in what they say. "Nobody at school likes me, everybody hates me, they all make fun of me." Those kinds of statements indicate victim training in progress. Or if the child is becoming a bully, you know that underneath he is feeling very helpless, like a victim, and is using persecution to avoid feeling the pain.

7

A person can move throughout this triangle of roles himself, without needing other players. For example, let's say you feel out of control with food, like a helpless victim. You decide that you are going to rescue yourself by going on a diet. When it doesn't work, you become angry. You begin to persecute yourself by feeling guilty and putting yourself down. After you have persecuted yourself enough, you end up right back in the victim position, feeling helpless and more out of control than ever. So you can jump around that circle yourself and don't even need anyone else to play the game with you.

The victim triangle becomes addictive. People who are victims will always attract rescuers and persecutors. If you don't have anyone to play the game with you, you will soon find someone. When you attract a mate, or friend, or neighbor, you are sure to link up with someone ideally suited to playing the game with you. It's just incredible how we are like magnets. You can go into a crowded room, if you are a victim, and a rescuer will suddenly appear and you feel an overpowering "magnetic attraction" almost instantly. It never fails. You can tell what is happening in your consciousness by the people that you attract into your life. If you have a lot of victims in your life, you can be sure that you are a rescuer.

When I first started doing therapy and counseling, I was definitely a rescuer. I had come from a family where my role was to take care of everyone. Each night after work I would feel stressed out because I was taking on everybody's problems. All night long I would be worrying about how I could help everybody. After a few years I needed to take a leave of absence because the pressure was getting to be too much. I went on a trip around the world and ended up in India. What I found after several years of meditation and studying higher consciousness was that it was not up to me to solve everyone's problems. I needed to let go of that rescuing role and just become a facilitator for others in their own healing process. Once I realized the difference between facilitating and rescuing, I could do therapy without being a rescuer. I share with others the tools that I have. I am present for them while they do their own healing, but the responsibility for their growth is up to them, not up to me. Most rescuers actually encourage the victim to remain dependent on them. So there is a mutually dependent relationship based on the victim roles. This codependency is the foundation of dysfunctional families and unhealthy relationships.

This codependency nearly always leads to addictive behavior. The most common feeling that the victim experiences is that of being out of control or powerless. The more helpless and out of control she feels, the more she tends to use drugs, food, and alcohol to keep numbing the pain.

When you feel out of control of your life, you also lose control of your habits. The powerlessness that you experience with food or drugs or alcohol is a manifestation of feeling out of control inwardly.

Almost everyone who comes in to the TRIM-LIFE weight release program that I developed has a background in a dysfunctional codependent family. The very first session of the class I ask them, "How many of you feel out of control with food?" Virtually everyone raises a hand. "How many of you feel that you have an addiction or compulsive behavior in your life?" Almost everybody does. This is true in almost any room I ask this question. Almost everybody has been caught in the circuit of this victim triangle, and has been taught to use these substances to numb their feelings and to dissociate from them.

Now let's explore some of these addictions. There are a lot of different types of addictive-compulsive behaviors. We've already mentioned tobacco, alcohol, and food. Another one is spending. Many people are compulsive spenders. Gambling is a very common addiction. Sexuality can be an addiction, too. You might wonder what a sexual addict is? A sexual addict is the same as a drug addict, that is, using a substance or a behavior to cover up feelings, to run away from emotions, to hide, to numb oneself from pain. I will give you a definition of addictive behavior from John Bradshaw, author of the book *Healing the Shame that Binds You:* "A mood altering event, experience, relationship or substance which initially gives you a euphoric feeling and later on leaves you feeling dependent, out of control and helpless. The purpose of it is to avoid feelings." That is what an addictive behavior is, and sexuality certainly is that for many people.

Another compulsive-addictive behavior is hypochondria. These people are addicted to being sick. They really test one's patience to not become the rescuer. Being a work-aholic certainly can be compulsive, too.

One of the most prevalent addictions is to unhealthy relationships. As we've been discussing, people can become addicted to codependent relationships and to the victim triangle. The person may be saying, "I really want to get rid of this guy," and they break up 25 times and they get back together 25 times. It's just like trying to give up cocaine. And it's exactly the same as the alcoholic who does well for a few months and then starts drinking again. People do well without each other and then they are back together fighting, hurting and abusing each other all over again and wondering why. Yet they keep re-creating the unhealthy relationship over and over again. It's because of that victim triangle; they are addicted to the dependency. That's what addictive behavior is all about: dependency.

9

The Victim Triangle
The Foundation of Codependency

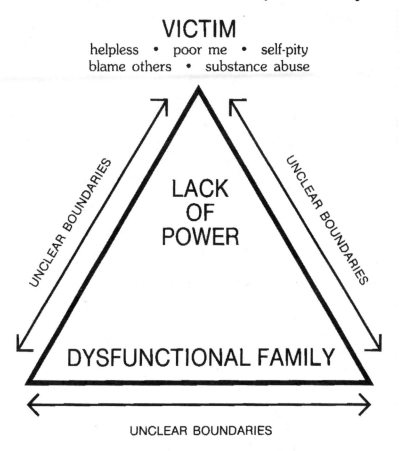

VICTIM
helpless • poor me • self-pity
blame others • substance abuse

LACK
OF
POWER

DYSFUNCTIONAL FAMILY

UNCLEAR BOUNDARIES

RESCUER
(VICTIM)

enabler
Martyr · suffers
discounts self · needs
guilt to control
avoids true feelings
over-stressed

PERSECUTOR
(VICTIM)

abuses others
guilt to control
withdrawal
use of drugs and alcohol

From Codependency to Health

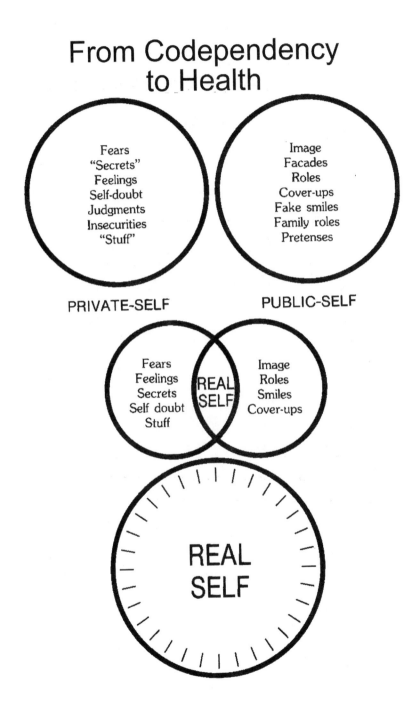

PRIVATE-SELF

Fears
"Secrets"
Feelings
Self-doubt
Judgments
Insecurities
"Stuff"

PUBLIC-SELF

Image
Facades
Roles
Cover-ups
Fake smiles
Family roles
Pretenses

Fears
Feelings
Secrets
Self doubt
Stuff

REAL SELF

Image
Roles
Smiles
Cover-ups

REAL SELF

The Dysfunctional Family

Chapter 2
The Victim Personality

For the victim every situation is a crisis: she's out in the middle of the ocean in a leaky boat and instead of patching up the leaks, she is continually bailing water.

Victims are basically persons who feel sorry for themselves! "Why does this always happen to me?" or "Poor me, nothing ever seems to go right!" You often have the feeling that everyone, or at least certain people, are always against you. You feel helpless and not in control of your own life. You are aware that on a deep level you feel inferior and that you do not really value yourself. You may find that you set your goals low and even then do not really expect to achieve them. You may also notice a lot of self-defeating behaviors.

Let's take a look at self-defeating behavior. Typically, you always stop short of your goals, such as dropping out of school before completing your degree, or getting drunk the night before a job interview. You're setting yourself up to lose. Another form of self-defeating behavior can be illnesses. One young woman always got migraine headaches just before final exams, giving her an acceptable excuse for not doing well. Another young man had allergies which always seemed to get between him and success. The psyche seems to be able to create many illnesses which the victim personality can conveniently use as an excuse.

The word "excuse" is a key in understanding the victim personality. If you have a victim personality, you will find yourself with a whole trunkload of excuses to fit any situation. In fact, you should be commended for the incredible creativity and imagination which you use to invent excuses or rationalizations for failure. The reason for the excuses is that consciously you do not believe that you want to fail. However, subconsciously you have been programmed to fail and you have been conscientiously trained to use excuses to rationalize each failure so that you do not really have to take responsibility for your failures.

The next step after the excuse is "blaming." You may notice that you usually blame others for your mistakes, problems or failures. Some victims even blame others for their whole lives being a disaster. The most common game here is called "If it Weren't for You ..." "If it weren't for you, I'd be happy!" or "... I'd be successful," or whatever. The blaming aspect serves to keep the victim feeling extremely helpless since it always

13

shifts the power onto someone else. After all, if you are powerless then whatever goes wrong in your life *has to be* someone else's fault.

The Blame Game is taught and played in families. Always looking for "whose fault it is," the children begin to think in terms of blaming others and not taking responsibility for their own behavior.

Children are very perceptive; they learn behavior as well as psychological games through imitation. They learn these games and then turn around and play them on the exact people (their parents) who taught them the games. Children not only imitate behavior, they imitate attitudes, ways of viewing life and self-identity. The victim personality is learned, reinforced and encouraged by their own family.

If you are a victim, you have been systematically taught "helplessness." Victim people may have incredible ability in the arts, or business, and yet there is always *something* that seems to hold them back. Very often it is drugs, alcohol or some type of addiction. Victim people tend to have addictive personalities, which means that they feel very dependent inside and are vulnerable to seeking "crutches." Victim family members often confuse love with pity. They go through life appearing weak in order to attract someone to rescue them (that is, pity and "save" them). To a victim, this is love.

Not all victims appear weak upon first meeting. I have met judges, doctors, businessmen, all of whom have appeared strong and confident, but were victims inside. In fact, victim personalities are found in all walks of life, ages, sexes and socioeconomic groups. But there are many common characteristics and certain phrases that can be used to detect the victim personality in yourself or in someone else. Psychological crutches are an instant giveaway. Alcoholics often describe how they feel out of control over the drug; this mirrors the way they feel about many aspects of their lives.

The Sieve Syndrome

The *Sieve Syndrome* is a subtle and intricate way of never succeeding, of continuing to remain helpless. If cleverly done, the failure never appears to be in the victim's control, but always appears to be due to "circumstances beyond his control." They always seem to be treading water. They are always patching up the leaky boats of their lives. To hear the victim tell it, no one else works as hard, has as many problems, or suffers so much bad luck! They continually feel overwhelmed by one crisis after another. They look so busy and yet they are running on a treadmill - never really getting anywhere except more entrenched in their own quicksand.

Kelly is an example of the Sieve Syndrome. When she divorced, she got two vehicles, child support, the farm, the daughter, the animals and the family home. Of course, as all victims do, Kelly still feels ripped off! She feels she is being "forced" to work and complains about her lack of time to get anything done. Many single mothers would feel blessed to have this situation in which Kelly earns $1,000 a month for working part-time, plus child support. And yet this young woman feels constantly overwhelmed.

As we look a little bit closer, we begin to see signs of the Sieve Syndrome. Kelly has been programmed to be a victim and the Sieve Syndrome serves well to reinforce this concept of herself. She's out in the middle of the ocean in a leaky boat and instead of patching up the leaks, she continues to bail water. Kelly views every situation as a crisis. If one does not exist, she has the uncanny ability to create another one. For example, she loves animals and is admired for her wonderful abilities with them. Actually, Kelly identifies with hurt stray animals (victims themselves) and continually tries to rescue them. This is another clue that the victim personality is operating. She often uses the plight of helpless or hurt animals to create crises in her own life.

Kelly makes elaborate plans for a weekend camping trip out of town with family members. The family is anxiously waiting for her and her daughter at a distant campsite. The ex-husband has been given very specific instructions about the importance of having the child there on time to leave for the trip. When he arrives to deliver the child he finds Kelly in a frantic state ... over a rabbit! All plans have been postponed now, the family is left unnotified at a remote campsite because a rabbit got stepped on by a horse!

Let's take a look now at how Kelly uses a simple project to create various crises (leaks in the boat) in her life.

She has a creative idea about a good way to save money on food next winter. She will raise rabbits to butcher for food. It sounds like an innocent project. But with her uncanny ability to victimize herself, Kelly is able to create situation after situation with the rabbits where she becomes victimized. She decides that she feels sorry for the rabbits (the pity factor) having to be in cages so she will let them out so they can "feel free" (a statement about her own sense of entrapment). Remember, she has purchased the rabbits to butcher, not as pets. So she lets the rabbits run free and, of course, then the problems begin. Almost daily there is some crisis in which a rabbit is getting hurt by a horse, chewed by a dog, or run

15

over by a car. To complicate what could have been a simple situation, the rabbits now begin to eat the neighbors' vegetable gardens.

The leaks in the boat are rapidly multiplying. The neighbors begin to come over and complain. This is how the victim produces her persecutors (see Victim Triangle diagram on page 10). Now Kelly can assume the innocent victim position.

"But I was only trying to keep these poor rabbits from being so closed up in those small cages," she explains innocently. The neighbor, also feeling victimized by Kelly's rabbits eating up his garden, is thinking of all his hard work down the drain. He is understandably angry and lets Kelly know how he feels. She then feels victimized by his anger and a continuing feud begins. The same situation then occurs with other neighbors who have planted gardens. So now more leaks in the boat are created. Just from this one small aspect of Kelly's life, she has set herself up for years of neighbor problems, feeling unsupported in a community that could have been supportive.

Now winter is approaching and Kelly begins to think about the need for wood. The boat is developing serious leaks now! If she had the support of neighbors, certainly there would have been some help from them. An even easier solution would have been for Kelly to have purchased the needed fuel. But that's not the way a true victim would handle this situation. Kelly decides she is going to go out in the woods herself and get the wood, a decision that creates a wonderful victim situation which she can maintain for most of the winter. People not showing up to help her, the truck breaking down, the chain saw not working - the list goes on. Kelly can maintain her image of the strong, liberated woman who does it all herself. This is a classic picture of a victim appearing to be strong to the outside world. But as you look closer at these victims you see how they create situations which make them appear to be overcoming major obstacles, when in fact those obstacles never had to be there in the first place.

It's very important to understand the blaming aspect of the victim's personality. Through the blaming, the victim always remains helpless and feels no responsibility whatsoever for the constant leaks in the boat. Let's look at Kelly again. If you were to talk to her about the situation, she would justify it by saying, "My neighbors are very insensitive people who really don't care at all about animals" (referring to the rabbits). In this way she makes a false assumption based on her own inappropriate behavior which caused their reaction in the first place. The definition of a person who is unable to see the forest for the trees applies in these cases. The victim wears an incredible set of blinders which block out just about

16

everything except for her own narrow view of the world. It is this continual blaming of others or outside forces which maintains the victimization. In her book *Irregular People*, Joyce Landorf refers to people who are emotionally blind, a perfect description of the victim!

Tom is another example of the Sieve Syndrome. Like many victims, he is a highly creative and talented person who never seems to get his life in order enough to do much with his talent. He sings, writes beautiful music, plays every instrument he comes in contact with, and understands the technical aspects of music. Tom was programmed by his family to become a victim and has fulfilled the familial expectations to a tee. He grew up watching his mother's victimization by his dad, in the form of physical abuse, humiliation and constant put-downs. Tom then became the target for his father's criticism and eventual beatings. The father's justification for the beatings was that he wanted his son to be perfect.

Each member of this family identifies with being a victim; the father was victimized as a child by his own father. He and Tom's mother proceeded to have seven children, which enabled them to continue to take the victim position of never being able to make ends meet.

Tom's mother felt pity for Tom and began to rescue him as a child. First, he was born needing corrective surgery on his feet. When a mother pities a child, it teaches self-pity to the child. Her pity for him increased when the father began to physically abuse him. And so in this way the family game of "Victim, Rescuer, and Persecutor" is taught to the child. The mother looks at him with pity and says "I love you" …. "poor Tom" - thus confusing love and pity.

Take time with the questionnaire on the following page to become more clear about how blame is at work in your life and how you can eliminate blame from your life.

BREAKING FREE FROM THE VICTIM PATTERN:
Eliminating the Blame

1. Who have you been blaming for this problem?

2. Are you willing to see that you have choices? Y/N (Circle)

3. List some choices you have to change this situation:
    a.

    b.

    c.

4. Once you begin to take back your power of choice, are you willing to see that some totally new choices may suddenly open up to you? Y/N (Circle)

List what those could be:

    a.

    b.

    c.

    d.

Chapter 3
The Victim Triangle

In every victim relationship, the basic underlying dynamic is two
victims, each blaming their feelings of helplessness and
inadequacy on the other.

The victim game is a family game that any number and combination of
people may play. The first basic assumption is that all members who
participate identify in some form with being a victim. Take Tom's family,
for example. Tom is the victim; he is young, helpless, has physical
problems and his mother feels sorry for him. So, the mother begins to
rescue Tom. She overprotects him, doesn't allow the other children to play
rough with him, and doesn't allow him to take risks. This makes Tom feel
even more helpless and sets him up to be resented by the other family
members who may persecute him. Then it is the father who begins to
persecute Tom. As the father sees his son being "pampered," he begins to
fear the boy will become a "sissy." To prevent this, the father begins to
"get tough" with the little guy. He feels it's time to teach him to be a man.
In this way, the father begins to persecute young Tom. The more the father
persecutes, the more the mother rescues and the more helpless and
confused young Tom feels. This is how codependency begins.

The victim triangle now becomes a vicious cycle. The father turns on
the mother and begins to persecute her for rescuing Tom. At this point the
mother becomes the victim, and Tom, feeling sorry for his mom, tries in
his way to rescue her. As soon as he turns into the rescuer, he will be
persecuted again. This is extremely upsetting to the child because Tom
doesn't fully understand the rules of psychological games yet. But he is
already quite adept at playing. Children are very perceptive and they learn
psychological games as easily as ring-around-the-rosie. They learn by
imitation and reinforcement.

So a child who grows up in a household involved in playing the victim
game learns very early to become a victim. In fact, the child becomes an
expert at finding variations of the game and seeking out other players.
Victim children most often will find *persecutors*, and then they can always
count on the mother to be the *rescuer* in the game. The victim child will
often get beaten up, pushed down or thrown over by some bully and come

home crying or with a black eye. His motive is to get "rescued" by mom; to the child this is love.

As the victim child grows, he learns to create more and more situations in which he is victimized, hurt, put down, abused, ridiculed, overpowered and rejected. The reason he is so proficient is because he has been classically conditioned by the rescuer in the family. Every time he is hurt or victimized, he gets attention (reinforcement) from someone who feels sorry for him.

It is important to realize that in the *Victim Family*, love and pity are interchangeable. So he gets reinforced with what he thinks is love but is actually pity. Think of a child you may know who is like this. It will help you to understand how many thousands of times in their young lives the game gets reinforced and they never seem to tire of playing it.

A victim child's favorite statement is "Nobody likes me." This is an attempt at trying to pull a reaction from the rescuer such as "Oh, poor Tommy," and he can wallow around in self-pity. If someone responds with "I like you," the victim immediately replies, "No you don't, nobody does." The victim becomes so good at evoking pity, which he interprets as love, that he begins to do it with teachers and strangers on the street or clerks in the store. It is a game and the victim can "sense" who will play from a mile away. It is not a conscious action, but automatic, i.e., subconscious.

As the victim grows, rejection becomes familiar, a way of life. Through rejection the victim can gain the most sympathy. Of course, the rejection is blamed on the other person. Never in their *wildest dreams* do they imagine that they may actually be soliciting that rejection. They actually create situations in which the other person, no matter how much love that person has, is forced to reject them. The victim is also very clever at seeking out people who have difficulty in forming close relationships or people who are in some other way unavailable.

The Rescuer

Hazel is a rescuer. That was the role assigned to her in her family by both her parents, but especially by her father. It goes back to parents who keep their marriage together "for the sake of the child." It therefore becomes the child's responsibility to "keep the marriage together." No wonder she became a rescuer. Hazel became the family "social worker," trying to keep the peace and ease the hurt and pain that her parents were intent on inflicting on each other.

Actually, she came from a long line of victims, as do most people who find themselves trapped in the triangle. First of all, being Jewish, she came from an ethnic background of suffering. The Jewish culture is filled with a heritage of centuries of suffering, victimization and persecution. Luckily there is also a great strength and sense of overcoming which has helped many Jewish people to triumph over the patterns of victimization. Furthermore, the Jewish culture does not hold the copyright on suffering and guilt. The Catholics and Italians run a close second, with every culture contributing its own unique style of victimhood.

Hazel had a long line of grandparents who taught her how to suffer diligently. One of the most important tools in the victim game is guilt. Hazel's parents, having learned directly from them, were adept at guilt trips. Victims use guilt to manipulate others to feel bad, feel sorry, and to ultimately get what they want. Guilt is used to control.

Hazel feels that her dad is a master victim and a master at the art of using guilt to manipulate. She states that when she would stand up to her mother and tell her how she felt, her dad would take her aside and tell her to be careful about what she said because her mom might have a heart attack! That would make her feel guilty and she would switch from telling her mother the truth to rescuing her and feeling sorry for her. A victim is very good at using guilt to turn anger into pity. For example, Hazel's mother caught her father having an affair and she was about to leave him. In the true victim spirit, her dad made a suicide attempt. Instant switch from persecutor to victim - a mighty convenient little tool! This left Hazel feeling responsible for her poor mother as well as her father. She has been a compulsive rescuer ever since, but is also very adept at switching quickly from one position to another.

The ability to switch roles and relationships in an instant is a very unique quality of the victim. It's kind of like the old "bait and switch" routine that some con men play. Or, as in the movie "The Sting," it is akin to The Big Con. It's important to note that most people who play the victim game seriously, also play it as a pastime too.

Hazel and her husband Gary are in their 70s. Hazel plays a hard-core game of rescuing *everyone*. She spent most of her life as a social worker taking on as many problems as her shoulders could carry. The way she usually operates is to feel sorry for someone, volunteer to do something for them, and then begin to feel burdened by what she has volunteered to do. As the burden becomes heavier, her resentment grows. Then she shifts from rescuer to victim. She does this by blaming the person she was rescuing for being such a burden. In this way she has made the person she was rescuing become the persecutor and she jumps down to being the victim. As you can see, it's quite a crafty little maneuver.

There was the time that Hazel and Gary volunteered to rescue some poor lonely German students. Hazel offered her home as a "host family" for two months. No one asked her to do it and she had never met the students. Months in advance, she began preparing for their arrival by cleaning, painting and fixing. Hazel cleaned the whole house from top to bottom and then decided the kitchen needed painting. While doing this she hurt her foot and was laid up for a while. Here is where the bait and switch takes place. She hurt her foot and now became the victim instead of the rescuer. She began to resent the students, whom she still has not even met and who certainly never asked her to do any of the cleaning and fixing.

Hazel's resentment grew as she decided that since her foot was hurt, she would have to hire someone to paint the kitchen for her. As it turned out, the job cost $500. More resentment. She then began to calculate all the money it would cost them to feed the students (never checking to find out if she was expected to feed them). She was feeling more and more victimized by the day, never realizing that she and she alone had created this entire situation from beginning to end. Then she found out that the students would be spending most of their time at the University and became even more aggravated, because she had gone to all this trouble for them and they didn't even appreciate it enough to stay at home. *Here comes the guilt!*

It gets more bizarre. One night, Hazel and Gary are driving to visit their son. On the way Hazel spots a "poor" young man waiting for a bus. She makes Gary stop to offer him a ride. He declines, saying that the bus will be there any minute and that the bus will let him off right near his home. Rescuers do not like their rescue attempts to be thwarted, so Hazel persists. She convinces the young man that they will take him home and that it is too late, too dark, too drizzly for him to have to wait for a bus. After much insistence, he reluctantly gets in the car. After driving for some time, Hazel mentions that they just have to make a short stop at their son's house, which she had completely neglected to tell the unsuspecting stranger. The son's house is considerably out of the way of the young man, and in an area where the bus lines don't even run. The stranger offers to take a bus or even a cab rather than wait (the poor guy just wanted to get home) but Hazel insists that they will be right out.

While visiting with their son and speaking about the poor young man in the car, they begin analyzing why he is out in the rain on a night like this. They somehow reach the conclusion that he is gay (purely speculation). They suddenly become incensed at the idea of a gay man being in their car. Gary, being prejudiced against gays, found this a justifiable reason to persecute an innocent stranger. Here is the "switch" from rescuer to victim to persecutor all in one swift instant. They angrily go out to the car, drive about 5 blocks away and drop him off out in the boondocks in the middle of the night.

Since they perceive now that he is gay and because of that he has somehow taken advantage of them, they feel justified in persecuting him. This incident shows that the victim game involves a "thought disorder" where perceptions are often confused or totally incorrect, but are accepted because they reinforce the individual's expectations, their "script." No doubt the young man is still wondering what that was all about!

Stress and the Rescuer

Suicide is, of course, the ultimate trip of the victim. It is the ultimate manipulation and the most poignant guilt trip possible. Many victims do not really want to die because then they would truly have to give up their suffering. Often they just save the threat or the attempt as the *coup de grace* to be used as needed. Some victims feel so helpless that they have even told me that they have tried many times to kill themselves and can't even seem to accomplish that. Now that's helpless!

The rescuer is a very important part of this triangle. The rescuer is the one who "appears" to be helping. However, what they are really doing is controlling by creating dependence. To stop rescuing would be to stop creating dependence: "Give a man a fish and he will eat for a day; teach him to fish and he can feed himself for the rest of his life."

The rescuer is usually a very dependent personality who has an intense need to be needed. So, for example, if a mother in a family is the rescuer, she will likely be very overprotective and spend more time doing it *for* the child rather than teaching the child to do it for himself. The rescuer thrives on taking on burdens and having people need her.

John came in with an incredible amount of stress in his life. He'd had two heart attacks by the age of 45. He had migraine headaches and severe neck, shoulder and back pain. This could be called *The Christ Complex* - a martyr carrying "the Cross" around on your shoulders. John is also 30 pounds overweight and wonders why his life is so stressful. In his first age regression it was discovered that John came from a "victim family" and was carefully programmed to take the role of the rescuer.

The rescuing personality develops in a victim family when a child is given too much responsibility at a young age, especially if the child perceives this as emotional responsibility, or feels overwhelmed[2]. John, who was the eldest son, is a good example. At age six, he was given full responsibility for his three-year-old brother. In a victim family, this creates a rescue situation. So one day John was in charge when the younger brother got hit by an automobile. He was blamed, of course, and immediately began a lifetime of feeling that if he just were "more responsible" it would never have happened.

John has experienced a lifetime of guilt and stress. Not only is he trying to be "more responsible" because of the incident with his brother, he also feels responsible for his father's pain. His father was a victim who never quite achieved success. John, labeled as "the responsible one," interpreted this label as meaning he was responsible to solve all the family pain. So each time he perceived his father as being unhappy, distressed or helpless, he began to feel the stress of "solving" this problem.

This pattern continued throughout his life, "feeling responsible" for situations that were in no way his fault. An example was working in a bank during a time of economic recession. People were losing money on investments and John went home each night with unbelievable tension in his neck and shoulders. In a hypnosis session it became obvious that John was emotionally rescuing all the bank customers. He was taking responsibility for their lives, their money and for the recession. No wonder he was in pain!

In his current job, John is the general manager of a fruit processing plant. He is again experiencing stress and has had two pre-heart attacks. Again John is taking responsibility for other people's problems. The growers had a bad season due to weather and yet John's rescuing personality feels he is somehow responsible.

It's very important to recognize here the difference between true responsibility and rescuing. True responsibility reflects the individual's ability to feel powerful in solving his own problems. It also involves the Serenity Prayer from Alcoholics Anonymous: "God, grant me the serenity to accept the things I cannot change, the courage to change the things I can, and the wisdom to know the difference." The rescuer usually feels helpless in changing his life, so he seeks the power by taking on the problems of others. This is also a manipulation, because it takes the attention or focus off of the rescuer's problems and puts it on someone else.

Therapists are themselves an obvious class of rescuers. Many have spent their whole lives focusing on other people's problems, often to the neglect of their own. Doctors and nurses are frequently in the same category. There has been much written about the high stress levels and burn-out among these professionals. In fact, recently we have learned that many physicians are using drugs and alcohol to deal with their stress.

In the book *The Hardy Executive,* authors Maddi and Kobasa talk about "hardy" personalities and their ability to grow from stress. The victim and the rescuer are often the same as an unhardy personality, persons who may end up with all kinds of stress-related illnesses. The reason is simple: the rescuer takes on other people's burdens as well as his own. Not only does he take on these problems, but he suffers as if they really were his responsibility to solve. The pay-off for the rescuer is the suffering. Remember, the victim manifests in three forms: the victim, the rescuer and the persecutor, the essential components of the victim triangle.

The Hardy Executive relates the unhardy personality as one who sees life as a burden rather than a challenge and who feels out of control rather than in control of things. This is the same as the victim and rescuer; every situation is one more straw on the back of that camel about to break. The rescuer assumes that someone up in heaven is keeping track of the straws and somehow the more straws (burdens) borne, the quicker or more certainly he will be rewarded. It's like earning brownie points up in the sky.

The typical rescuer is The Martyr Mother who takes on the problems of everyone in the family and suffers continually. In fact, this person wouldn't know what to do if she wasn't suffering. She can sit and tell you all the sob stories of the family and how she is trying to find help for all of them. One son is a dope dealer who just got arrested, the daughter's husband just left her with three kids, and her niece was killed in a car accident. She spends much of her waking day trying to get the dealer out of jail, the daughter a new husband and the deceased into heaven.

Actually, she has created the victim situations that her children are in. Since she has been rescuing them since childhood, they have learned helplessness. Because of her strong need to be needed, she has been washing their clothes, cleaning their rooms, cooking their food, ironing, and maybe even doing their homework for them. She hasn't taught them to do it; she has done it for them. There is a world of difference between the two.

The rescuer has an incredible need to be needed. She will often take the position of the go-between. She is everyone's friend and takes on the responsibility of keeping everyone happy.

Tom's mother, Sally, is a prime example of a rescuer. She goes back and forth between the father, who is a persecutor, and the children trying to keep everyone happy and most of all making sure she is needed. In fact, the rescuer will often stir things up and then jump in and rescue to insure being continually needed, creating job security as a rescuer.

Another example is Dan's mother Fran. When Dan was a child, Fran played a hard-core game of rescuer. Dan began loving and trusting his mother as all children do. The father was a persecutor (which we will get into later in more detail). So when the father would come home from work, the mother perceived that the father was looking for information about the child. He felt all children needed discipline. Fran, needing to be needed by all, would tell the father about the things little Dan had done which needed discipline. Dad would then spank, intimidate or otherwise humiliate little Dan. Then Fran would step in and rescue little Dan from Dad. Here Dan was the victim, Dad the persecutor and the entire scene a set-up by Fran the rescuer.

Soon little Dan became aware that he was being betrayed by his mother and began to pull away from her. Of course, this threatened her and the game intensified. Fran became more secretive in betraying the boy to his dad, and the punishments became more severe. Fran felt more needed by little Dan as he became more and more victimized by the father.

Other rescuers will go outside the family to rescue victims, even at the expense of their own family members. As a young woman, Hazel was a social worker, a professional rescuer. Working with the deprived, the helpless, and the down-and-outs, Hazel would often enlist her family to rescue her clients. Many times her family would have nothing to say about whether or not they were willing to participate in the rescues. There was no questioning Hazel's rescue plans.

Two of Hazel's clients were old ladies who lived together and were on welfare. She decided what they needed and who was going to provide it for them. First of all, she decided that they needed children around to play and bring some joy into their lives. So every Saturday, Hazel would bring her two boys over and drop them off to "entertain" the two old ladies. The boys hated this and felt uncomfortable in the home of these strangers. The boys wanted to be out playing with their friends, but their mother was using them as pawns in her rescue game.

One day, Hazel decided that the two old ladies needed wood for the winter. She took it on as her responsibility and then enlisted her husband and sons to do the work. So her husband Gary spent many hours locating a truck to borrow and then he and the boys spent a whole weekend cutting, loading and stacking the wood for the ladies. Hazel then proudly took the credit as the two old women thanked her.

It's important here to understand the nature of the rescue and the motives. The motives are anything but altruistic! Hazel is rescuing these ladies because she, herself, feels so helpless. To rescue someone else makes her feel more powerful. Also, the enlisting and control of others in her "projects" gives her an even stronger sense of power. The "helpless old ladies" merely reflect how she feels about herself. Also, the use of guilt to manipulate her family to participate in her rescues is far from healthy for them. It's important to recognize how destructive the use of guilt is.

Another motive of the rescuer is that she often has an intense fear of rejection. So she will usually take the role of the *Placater* in the family or among friends. The rescuer/placater is often two-faced, telling each side exactly what she thinks they want to hear. So, as in the case of Dan, the mother would tell the dad what she thought he wanted to hear, which was how bad little Dan had been. She would then tell little Dan what she thought he wanted to hear, that she loves him. She would try to comfort him after the dad has spanked him, then later go to the dad and tell him how glad she is that he is taking care of the discipline since she is so poor at that kind of thing.

The main motive of the placater is that she doesn't ever want anyone to be mad at her, so she diverts everyone's anger away from herself and onto someone else. This is a very destructive game to play with children who trust their mothers to protect them from harm, not lead them into it. Talk about a stab in the back!

The placater is ubiquitous in alcoholic families. All alcoholic families play some form of the victim game. Quite often, the father is the alcoholic (victim and persecutor) and the mother is the rescuer. The mother tries to "help" the dad, but actually enables him to drink. She covers up for him, may give him money for alcohol, and "pretends" to the children. She constantly walks around on eggshells trying very hard not to do anything that will set him off. So she placates him. This is what we call an "emotional rescue." She tells him what she thinks he wants to hear in order to keep from setting off a drinking binge. When the alcoholic binges, he will commonly blame it on someone else, usually the closest rescuer.

The most destructive aspect of all this is that the children are watching and listening. They learn by imitation. So the children are learning to play rescuer by not being assertive and by walking around on eggshells. They are often enlisted to rescue the rescuer (the mother) when she is persecuted by the alcoholic victim. The cycle grinds on, and perpetuates itself with another generation.

The Persecutor Personality

The persecutor is the aspect of the victim that lashes out because of feeling so inferior, helpless and out of control. The persecutor turns that fear into anger and blames everyone and everything for his problems. That is one of the reasons he feels so helpless - he is constantly giving away his power. He gives responsibility to everyone else around him rather than taking that responsibility himself. Then he lashes out in anger at the abuse he thinks is being hurled at him. Actually, the abuse or victimization is exactly what he does to others and subconsciously encourages others to do to him. In very subtle ways, he teaches others how to treat him. It goes back to the "sweatshirt" concept in the book *Games People Play*. He wears the metaphorical sweatshirt that says, "Kick me."

The persecutor quite often was himself a victim as a child and was persecuted by an adult or older sibling in his family. So he learns the technique of taking out his anger and frustration on others who are weaker than he is. Though often cloaked with the guise of discipline, it is actually just a way for a weak person to feel stronger. The abusive parent is a prime example of a persecutor personality. The incredible need to prove his strength by taking out his anger on children is quite pathetic. And, tragically, the damage done to the children is profound.

An example of this is Tom's dad, Harry, who was horribly abused as a child but never spoke of it to anyone. In fact, he claimed to remember nothing of his background; repression is quite prevalent in these situations. Harry began by abusing his wife in front of the children. This was so intimidating to the children that they became filled with fear and insecurity; fear that dad will hurt or kill mom and then they will be left alone with him, unprotected. Fear and anxiety in children is often labeled "hyperactivity." So the child who is the most filled with fear about being abused will often become hyperactive and will indeed be "disciplined" or abused for this behavior which he often has no control over. This is a self-fulfilling prophecy: the exact thing that is feared the most will be realized. This is precisely what Tom created in his life. Fearing that his dad would do the same abusing to Tom that had been done to his mother, Tom became anxious and began to "act out." His dad began to beat him for his behavior. The more anxious he became, the less control he had over his behavior, and the more punishment he received. In other words, "the harder he tried to be good," the worse he behaved. The other children hid in the closet when Tom was being beaten because they could not bear to watch.

Take time with the questionnaire on the following pages to become more clear about the victim patterns at work in your life.

Victim Triangle Self Diagnosis Test

Do you wonder if you have "Victim Patterns" in your life? Take this test and see for yourself.

1. I feel out of control in one or more of these areas of my life (T or F)

    _____Food
    _____Alcohol
    _____Drugs
    _____Money
    _____Discipline of children
    _____Relationship with spouse or lover
    _____Work
    _____Stress
    _____Tobacco
    _____Other

2. When I feel out of control, I tend to blame others (T or F)

    _____My children
    _____My spouse or lover
    _____My boss
    _____My co-workers
    _____The weather
    _____My parents
    _____The government
    _____Other

3. One or more of my family members thinks suffering is a virtue (T or F)

    _____Mother
    _____Father
    _____Spouse
    _____Myself
    _____Sisters
    _____Brothers
    _____Grandmother
    _____Grandfather

4. I often feel sorry for myself (T or F)
   Reason: _____

   _____

5. I often feel sorry for others (T or F)

   _____Son
   _____Daughter
   _____Mom
   _____Dad
   _____Spouse or lover
   _____Friend
   _____Other

6. My children often engage in "Poor Me" attitudes (T or F)

7. I help people sometimes to a fault; i.e., sometimes my own family suffers so that I can help someone else (T or F)

8. I often feel sorry for hurt or stray animals or children and want to take them home (T or F)

9. I often feel like a martyr (T or F)

10. An important member of my family is a martyr (T or F)

11. I have a lot of guilt feelings in my life (T or F)

12. I find myself using guilt to try to control my children (T or F)

13. Bad things always seem to happen to me or my family (T or F)

14. I work hard but never seem to be appreciated (T or F)

15. No one ever notices the good things I do (T or F)

16. People are always picking on me (T or F)

17. My parents used guilt to control me (T or F)

18. I was a victim of child abuse (T or F)

_____Physical
_____Sexual
_____Emotional

19. There was violence in my family (T or F)

_____Physical
_____Emotional

20. One or both of my parents had an alcoholic problem when I was growing up or has one now (T or F)

21. One or both of my grandparents has had an alcohol problem (T or F)

22. My _____ felt sorry for me because _____

_____ (T or F)

Score 10 points for each true and 1 for each check mark.

Score 40-50: You have the victim syndrome in your life and should seek treatment.

50-60: The victim pattern is very strong and treatment is recommended to prevent stress-related illness.

over 60: You are deeply entrenched in the victim triangle, and immediate treatment is essential in preventing further disasters in your life!

Chapter 4
The Victim Triangle and Sexual Abuse

To love ourselves is the opposite of being selfish. Feeling good inside is like having a well filled with love: we have so much more to give others. You can't draw water from an empty well; when there is self-hate and insecurity inside, that is all we have to give to others.

The Hobbs Family

Many families who have been involved in a cycle of abuse confuse fighting with intimacy. It's the only way they know to become intimately involved with each other. The Hobbs family is a clear demonstration of this. The story begins in 1984 when Harry and Carole brought their two young daughters into my office. They had been sexually abused by Harry's brother, Dave. Harry and Carole were furious. How could Dave have done this to their children? They felt used, since the two families had been very close and they felt Dave had used that friendship to get to the kids. As the therapy began, it became obvious that there was also physical abuse in the family. Harry had an uncontrollable temper. In fact, the youngest daughter Margaret came to sessions sitting on a "donut" due to a spinal injury. She was in constant pain. She reported that her dad used to kick her in the butt with the steel-reinforced toe of his boot. This was emotionally humiliating as well as physically damaging.

After many months of counseling it became quite obvious that the father was a "tyrant" and the source of much unhappiness in the family. Even though Carole loved him dearly, it was difficult for her to sit by and watch the physical and emotional abuse of her children. When she confronted Harry, he turned his anger on her or went out and got drunk. Harry was extremely defensive in counseling and everyone walked around on eggshells when he was in the session. I had to be particularly careful not to threaten his precarious ego.

The victim game played by this family became obvious the longer the consultation went on. They confused love with pity. They played the rescue game by feeling sorry for animals, children and anyone they perceived as an underdog. They actually wanted to take in foster children when they couldn't even deal with their own problems. Each member felt like a victim and went round and round upon the triangle. Harry obviously was a victim and there was a hint that perhaps he had been abused in his family. He was baffled, however, to realize that he could recall nothing from his childhood.

Harry and the older daughter Brenda were intensely involved in conflict. Brenda played the victim which was totally inappropriate. She was a beautiful, extremely intelligent and popular young girl. Yet being trained in the victim tradition, she could always find ways to make herself the underdog, to solicit the pity which she confused with love.

Therapy ended abruptly when Harry interpreted that he was being blamed for all the family problems. His perception was probably correct. Once his male ego had been stepped on, no amount of coaxing from the family could get Dad back to the sessions. I found it extremely frustrating. But as it turned out, this was not the end of therapy for this family.

About a year and a half later, I received a phone call from the younger daughter, Margaret. She indicated on the phone that her dad was sexually abusing her. I was shocked and upset; he had been so self-righteously upset about the same actions of his brother. I contacted Carole, the mother, to inform her and see what could be done about getting Harry in for treatment. Carole was dubious whether this was going to happen.

After several weeks, I finally received a phone call from Carole. She wanted to make an appointment for Harry. She said that at first he said no, but later on he reluctantly said yes. I felt that if Harry could get over the bad feelings he had left counseling with, he could utilize therapy to deal with the current crisis.

Harry entered my office uptight and embarrassed. I quickly reassured him that there were no judgments on my part, and that I just wanted to do whatever I could to help the family deal with this situation. He said that coming into my office about this was probably the hardest thing he had ever done. He said that he was terribly afraid to come and yet he realized he was more afraid not to.

Harry is a farm boy. He is a simple person, down to earth and very likable. The reason I say "boy" is that behind that beard is a boyish grin and a childlike twinkle in his eye; not someone you would think of as a child-molester. But today the twinkle was gone, replaced by a troubled, fearful inquisitiveness. He was desperately trying to understand what was happening. He stated that he wasn't aware of molesting the girls, but yet he knew that they wouldn't lie about something like that. He was terribly confused.

I could see that talking about this with the conscious mind was not going to get us very far, especially when he told me that he had no recollection *whatsoever* about his childhood. I told him that I wished to use hypnosis to get to the bottom of this. He was hesitant but willing.

Hypnosis is really the most effective way to deal with this type of situation. The conscious mind was obviously blocking out the information which we were searching for, and we would have to bypass the conscious mind to get to the subconscious. Since the subconscious is considered to be 90% of the mind, there was an enormous amount of material that Harry was concealing from himself. It was most likely too painful for him to remember.

Therapy Begins

Harry immediately went into a deep state of hypnosis and we began by going back to the most recent time he felt sexually attracted to his daughters. Hypnotherapy works best when you can focus in on one specific feeling. He was able to focus in on this feeling, even though on the conscious level he had totally denied experiencing a sexual feeling for his daughters. As we went back, he described several occasions of playfulness where he and Margaret were playing and wrestling. He was curious how she would react if he touched her "boob" and so he did. These feelings again were much more childlike or child-to-child than adult-to-child. On one occasion he saw her in the kitchen and wondered what it would be like to grab her "boob." He did, and she smacked him.

With his other daughter Brenda, the attraction was not quite so playful, although the childlike curiosity remained. I told his subconscious mind to return to the beginning of this problem. The subconscious mind is like an incredible computer. It can automatically select the information which you request.

All of a sudden, Harry was a baby. He was in his crib and being molested by his older sister. He was crying and reliving the whole experience right there before my eyes. "Leave me alone, stop, you're hurting me," he was crying. Over and over again he cried, "Leave me alone!" His voice and tone were those of a child, a small child. I then took him to the next situation and he was not much older, perhaps one or two years old. He was having his diaper changed - the older kids were sucking on him. It made him feel uncomfortable.

He then got older. He was in bed with his brothers. There were many children and few beds. The boys all slept together. The brothers began touching him, sucking on him and then forcing him to suck on them. He gagged and choked - "No more, stop, yuck, leave me alone!" I asked, where are your parents? "In the field," was always the response. In the bed, each one of the older boys took turns with him. He had become the victim - they were the persecutors, the victimizers. He was totally at their mercy. He was the youngest, with no one there to protect him.

Harry got a little older in the next regression and realized that none of the older kids really liked him. They were all angry because he was the youngest, "the baby." He wanted their love. "Why don't they like me? I want them to like me."

He went back to a scene where he and his daughter Brenda were out in the fields waiting to bale hay. Suddenly, he was right there. "Hey Brenda, what would you do if someone tried to touch you?"

"I'd kick them in the balls," replied Brenda.

Hmm, I wonder if she really would, Harry thought.

Beginning to feel sexually aroused, and curious at the same time, Harry continued to contemplate the idea. Suddenly, he grabbed the breast of his fourteen-year-old stepdaughter. She didn't know how to react; she was upset and confused, and walked away to be alone with her feelings. Harry was now excited, intrigued. "Well, she didn't kick me in the balls. I wonder if she liked it?"

Harry's thoughts now turn to his younger, more voluptuous natural daughter Margaret. "I wonder how Margaret would react if I did the same to her?" In the hypnosis session, Harry regressed to a scene where he was in the kitchen and Margaret walked through. He reached out and grabbed her breast; she clobbered him over the head. Harry laughed and thought, *Hmm, an interesting reaction.*

I then suggested to Harry, "Let yourself go to another time when you had those same or similar feelings." Harry is now in Brenda's bedroom, to tuck her in and say goodnight. She is upset.

"Lay down with me and hold me," she requests of Harry, needing some parental comfort and reassurance.

"It's cold in here. I'll just get under the covers with you," he answers. Immediately, he begins to feel sexual arousal as he crawls under the covers with Brenda. He's excited, confused, and intrigued all at the same time. He begins to feel very uncomfortable, wisely concluding, "It's time to leave."

"I should tell Carole, but I'm scared to tell her. Why is this happening; where is this coming from?" he begs.

"Go back to the beginning, back to the source of this," I instruct him and begin tapping his forehead to take him back to his childhood. "Raise your finger, when a time or place comes into your awareness." His finger goes up. "How old are you there?" I ask.

"I'm four," he replies in a very small four-year-old voice. I wait. His body begins moving, his breathing becomes heavier. Harry is obviously agitated. "Stop," he begins to cry. "Leave me alone. I'm gonna tell Mom. Yes she will believe me."

"What's happening?" I query.

"It's Bobbie, she won't leave me alone, she's touching my peter."

"Where are your mom and dad?"

"They're gone to the fields. They're always gone to the fields."

"Is anyone else home?"

"No, Bobbie's baby-sitting me."

"How old is Bobbie?"

"She's 13."

Harry begins to cry again, "Leave me alone, stop! No more." He's writhing around as if trying desperately to get away from someone. He then curls up into a fetal position - it's the only safety he has as a four-year-old. Suddenly his arms snap back over his head. Brenda is holding his arms down so she can continue her sexual assault. "Leave my wiener alone. I'm going to tell Mom and then you'll be sorry." His arms are rigidly pressed into the couch as if the molestation were happening all over again.

"Go tell your mother," I instruct Harry. "Tell her how you feel."

"Mom, Bobbie was doing nasty things to me. She kept touching my wiener and wouldn't stop." He pauses, listening to her reply. "Yes she did," he moans loudly in his four-year-old voice. "Yes she *did!*" he screams emphatically.

A very heartbroken look crosses his face now as he realizes that Bobbie was right. "She doesn't believe me," he stammers. "She doesn't believe me." He draws his whole body back up into the fetal position again; the only safety available is returning to the womb.

The most important task now is to heal this abused, heartbroken child, to begin to re-parent that victim child and teach Harry how to do this for himself. Since there was no nurturing available to him as a child, that may not be an easy task. Without role models of proper parenting, Harry had nothing to draw from.

I instruct Harry one step at a time. "Bring your attention to that four-year-old that you were. Now, become the loving, nurturing parent to that child. Take him in your arms and hold him close. Let him know how much you love him, how special he is to you. Let him know that you have unconditional love for him. There are no strings attached to your love. He doesn't have to perform to receive your love: it's always there. And most of all, let him know that you are his protector. That you will always protect him if someone tries to hurt him. That you will always believe him and be there for him."

As I speak, Harry has his arms around himself, loving that child, loving himself. He is smiling and there is a warm glow in the room. I can feel his love for the child part of himself and this is the beginning of the healing process. "Do you love that child?" I ask.

"Oh, yes," he croons as if it is the most precious feeling he has ever experienced.

"Does the child take in your love?"

"Oh, yes," he coos again.

Harry is caressing the child as if he has never been held or cuddled before. He is fully immersed in this experience. I then ask him to get in touch with his "heart center" and feel God's love within him. He is easily able to do this, and an ever warmer glow fills the room. I can literally feel the healing taking place. I am making an audiotape of the healing process for him to take home. In this way, he can reinforce the process over and over again.

The subconscious mind works through repetition. And just as all the negative ideas happened over and over to Harry, the positive ones must be repeated to change the old responses. Habit responses are like grooves in a record; the more you play them, the deeper the grooves become. So by making a tape for Harry, he can begin to replace some of the negative grooves with positive ones.

I bring Harry back to the room, careful to be slow, gentle and give him some space. He has been in a very deep trance and it will take him some time to return to his conscious mind. I hold his hand and I can feel the love and gratitude in his heart. I can also see it in his eyes. We do not talk about the session, since it will take him many days or weeks to integrate all that has transpired during the past hour and a half.

We hug and he can feel my acceptance and support. His heart is open and there is an almost mystical closeness developing between us.

In two weeks Harry returns. He is a changed person. The fear is gone from his voice. He is more sure of himself and quietly announces, "I've remembered some other things." I was hoping that would happen; his subconscious mind was beginning to open up. I'm excited to see this process happening to a man who has told me he remembers nothing of his childhood. The story of his family now begins to unravel; the pieces of the puzzle are fitting into place.

"All of us fourteen children and two parents lived in a two bedroom cabin with an attic. There was a smaller cabin in the back for all of the boys. There was only one bed in the cabin, which we all shared in the summer. The lack of heat forced us into the attic in the winter. There was no heat there either, or plumbing. I remember running out to the outhouse in the middle of the night with snow on the ground. The girls all slept in one room also. The oldest boy is 21 years older than I am. Here is a list of the names from oldest to youngest: Floyd, Arnold, Ruth, Ralph, Art, Don, Ida, Nola, Carl, Bobbie, Burt, Edith, Linda, Harry. These original fourteen children have had 135 grandchildren for my parents and 70 great-grandchildren.

"Do you think that the incest in the family was started by an adult, either your mom or dad?" I ask.

"Not at all. I would be very surprised if that were the case. Since I was the youngest child, I knew Dad better than most of the children. I spent a lot of time with him after the others were gone. I can't imagine that he would have done anything like that. In fact, he was very strict concerning things like that. The girls had a dress code. They had to be fully dressed even in the summertime when it was very hot."

"What have you remembered?"

"Well, I remembered masturbating with my brothers Carl and Burt and some homosexual affairs with the neighbor kids Ron and Allen. The details are foggy, but I would like to know more."

We begin the hypnosis in the usual way. This time the images come easier and sooner. "Go back to your relationship with your brother," I said, tapping him on the forehead to help locate the proper information. "Let yourself get younger and younger now, going all the way back. You can feel your body shrinking down, getting littler and littler, smaller and smaller. You can feel your arms getting smaller, your legs getting smaller. Going all the way back to the source of these feelings with your brothers. When a time, a place or a situation comes to you, just say I'm here."

"I'm here," replies that child-voice.

"How old are you now?"

"I'm three."

"What's happening there?"

"I can't find anyone. No one's around." His voice changes from a cheery three-year-old to a lonely, scared child. "No one's here."

"Where is everyone?"

"They're all in the field. Carl's supposed to be watching me today. Carl, where are you? Carl? Carl? Where are you?" He's upset, lonely, wandering around the house calling for his brother.

"Okay, let yourself go to the next time, the next scene that comes to you. When you're there, just raise your finger." The finger goes up.

"How old are you now?"

"I'm five," he says, sounding just a tiny bit older than he had at three.

"What's happening?"

"Carl and Burt are in the barn doing the chores. We've got a fort up in the hayloft where we play. I'm looking for them. They're up in the loft. Hey, what are you guys doing up there? They want me to come up. When I do, they kick down the ladder so I can't get back down. Hey, what are you doing?" There is a shocked quality in his voice now.

"What's happening?" I ask.

"They're playing with each other's wienies, you know, jacking off. Hey, I want to leave. I don't want to watch you guys doing that anymore. It makes me sick."

Carl and Burt begin now to turn their attentions to young Harry. "Come on, Harry, it's fun."

"It's not fun to me. Leave me alone."

"Come on, Harry, it feels so-o-o good."

"It doesn't feel good to me. Bobbie does it to me all the time. I don't like it. Leave me alone," he whines loudly. "Stop, leave me alone. I want to get down, put the ladder back."

"Let yourself go to the next time now," I suggest. He raises his finger. "How old are you now?"

"I'm five," the small voice responds. "We're in bed, Burt and Carl and I. No, I don't want to sleep in the middle. It's too hot in the middle. How come you guys always have to do that? Quit it! Quit touching me. No, I don't like it. It's not fun to me. I hate it when Bobbie does it and I hate it more when you do it. It does not feel good. I'm sleeping on the floor."

"They're crazy! They've been watching the cows too much. How dumb! Putting their wieners inside each other. They seem to like it. I wonder how it feels?" The five-year-old dozes off to sleep with the picture of his brothers in his mind.

"Now let yourself go to the next time," I instruct.

"I'm almost six now. Carl and me are up in the bedroom in the attic. Carl, he's playing with my wiener and his at the same time. Just leave me alone, Carl. No, I don't like that. Stop. Take your wiener out of me! That

40

hurts! Ow, you're hurting me! Stop, I'm going to tell. Carl, ple-e-e-ase stop!"

Harry rolls back up into the fetal position and begins to suck his thumb. He's again returning to the only secure place he's ever known - the womb.

"Why are you hiding?" I ask the fetal-positioned child.

"Because, I can't let them see me sucking my thumb. If I do, they make me suck their peters. It's yucky!"

The next picture that comes to Harry is in an old trailer in the wrecking yard. "I'm with my two friends, Ron and Allen. They are teaching me to play strip poker. I keep losing; they keep laughing. I keep having to take off more clothes. 'You guys must cheat, you never have to take off anything.' Now they want me to suck their wieners. They take turns sucking mine. What the heck, doesn't everybody?"

It's at this point in his young life that Harry gives up. Until now, he fought it. He resisted the sexual advances made by his brothers and friends. But now, some part of his brain has realized that there is no use fighting it. The sexual advances are so prevalent, so overpowering, so constant. And so Harry, at the age of 10, "joins the crowd."

I again complete the session having him be the loving, nurturing parent. He is learning to create a parent inside himself, one who was never there for him, that right now he can only imagine. Reprogramming the computer of his subconscious mind will make him healthier. Going back and attempting to correct the past through a mental re-creation will improve upon the present and future.

Harry comes out of his session and begins to talk about his family and their incredible lack of closeness. Even though as children they were sharing the most intimate parts of themselves with each other, as adults they greatly fear intimacy. Perhaps the fear is that, since in the past closeness inevitably led them to sex, closeness in the present would do the same. So they begin to build walls to protect themselves from their instincts. Unfortunately, the walls have become so thick and tall that they prevent even the slightest contact except on the most superficial level.

Harry begins to feel the impact now of what has actually transpired in his family. He's beginning to realize how far-reaching the effects are. He talks about the total lack of affection in his family, about sisters and brothers who, now as adults, do not hug or touch in any way, who are even afraid to hug their own children. He realizes his own fear of hugging his children was that it would stimulate sexual excitement. He then makes the next and most obvious conclusion: if I molested my children, probably many of my siblings did the same. There could be hundreds of children just in our family that have been sexually molested. His curiosity is not all that is now aroused. His anger is as well.

Chapter 5
The Victim Triangle and Family Abuse

Many people try to fill voids in their otherwise seemingly boring lives with drama *and* chaos. *Addicted to the drama, they confuse drama with intimacy. In fact, it is the continual drama which* prevents *true intimacy.*

The Codependent "Switch"

One day, I receive a phone call from Carole, Harry's wife. She somberly states that she must come in to see me. I sense a certain desperation in her voice and imagine that Harry's temper has gotten him in trouble again and that she is thinking of divorce.

Carole enters my office wearing a grim look. Even her usual self-conscious giggle is gone. I ask my usual, "Well, how are things going?"

She begins talking about Harry and how he seems to be recovering from all of this quite well. He's been getting stronger ever since our last session. He's feeling better about himself and has completely backed off from Brenda. He and Brenda are getting along better than ever and things are actually mellow around the house.

This is great news to me - a breakthrough! For the first time since I've worked with Harry, someone else besides the two of us could see the change. I feel elated. "Then why are you so upset?" I inquire. I couldn't understand why Carole wasn't as thrilled as I was since this is what we had all been working toward for so long.

She begins to slowly talk about how she was no longer losing weight the way she had been; in fact, she was eating compulsively again. Also, since all this had been coming to light with Harry and his family, her sexual desire for him had all but died. "I keep thinking about it when we make love and it's hard for me to get turned on."

She also describes an incident when their younger son torched a jar filled with gasoline and almost blew himself up.

We begin to do the hypnosis and I take her back to the last time she was eating out of control. "Get in touch with the feeling that immediately preceded the 'pig out'."

"Guilt," she replies. "I feel guilty for not being able to handle Harry's problem."

"What else are you feeling?" I ask. Immediately I begin to recognize the pitiful voice of the victim. "I'm tired of always being hurt. I'm tired of

43

always being the one who should give in no matter how much I've been hurt."

I begin to realize that the "switch" had just taken place between Carole and Harry. All during the time that Harry was dealing with "his victimization," he was the victim and Carole was the rescuer. Now that Harry was getting better, stronger, and more whole, Carole was dipping into the victim role and feeling weaker. It's as if they cannot both be strong at the same time. And the stronger one gets, the weaker the other one becomes. And the weaker one becomes, the stronger the other one becomes! A tragically perfect example of how codependency works.

"How have you been hurt?" I ask.

"Five years ago Harry had an affair with my best friend. It's interfered with the passion. I never felt I could talk to anyone about it." By now, Carole, who usually is quite controlled, is crying.

In the hypnotherapy session, I hand her a pillow and give her the instruction, "Talk to your friend and tell her what you're feeling."

"I just don't understand how you could do that to me! I thought we were as close as any two friends could be. You betrayed my trust in you and in the whole concept of friendship. I hate what you've done to me; you have robbed me of something that I can never get back."

I was beginning to see that Carole certainly had been hurt, but I still didn't get how she connected this with the incest in Harry's family or why she was still holding on to this hurt five years later. Part of the reason was that she had held it in for so long and had never dealt with it; but she told me at the beginning of the session that it was only recently she began to turn off from Harry. I decided to inquire. "Carole, talk to Harry now and tell him how this is related in your mind to the incest in his family."

"Helen is Dave's daughter-in-law!" she exploded. "All the hurt is compounded. Everything that has hurt me is related to his family. Now that he's resolved his feelings, he's wanting to spend more time with them. They make me sick and I can't stand to be around any of them."

"Talk to the whole family now, Carole, and tell them how you feel."

"You make me so sick, I could puke! You're constantly putting on all those airs about what righteous, God-fearing people you are - you're a bunch of *pukes!* You have totally destroyed my vision of what family is supposed to mean."

Carole's feelings are intense now and I wondered if she was including Harry in these feelings. If she felt his whole family was so disgusting, perhaps he disgusted her too. But it turned out I was wrong in that assumption.

44

"Harry, I want our happy sex life back. I want it to be the way it was before all this garbage entered our lives - or should I say before I knew about it. I know this isn't your fault, but I can't help but think that you're related to all these people. When I start thinking about this when we're in bed, a switch turns off and part of me feels dead."

I noticed that she wasn't disgusted by him. She was hurt and angry, and turned herself off for protection. She would have to realize that she is not a victim here and that she can turn that switch back on any time she wants to let go of all this. To stop being the victim she would have to find forgiveness and stop blaming Harry.

"Okay, Carole, now put yourself in Harry's shoes and say how he is feeling."

"It's not any one individual's fault; all of it was just handed down from one child to the other. I've forgiven them and myself, why can't you?"

Carole immediately responds to her version of Harry. "That's exactly why I feel guilty, because I know that intellectually, but I can't forgive or let go in my heart. If he can forgive them, why can't I?"

I had a feeling that the answer had to do with Carole now being in the victim role. The victim holds on to hurts as a freezing man clutches on to his coat in a snow storm. The hurts and pain become ammunition in the game, especially when victim jumps down to persecutor. This is Carole's subtle way of persecuting Harry for getting strong. Now the trick is to bring it to her awareness without her feeling that I am discounting her feelings.

"Carole, talk to Harry's family now and tell them what you can forgive them for."

As she begins to speak, I can hear the victim quality in her voice. That whiny, suffering, self-pitying sound is a certain clue that the victim is in operation. "I can't forgive you because I'm hurting too much. As long as I'm hurting, my whole family is hurting. All my children are hurting when I'm hurting. You've destroyed our whole family."

"Carole, do you feel like a victim now?" I ask gently.

"Yes," she replies in a child's voice, another unmistakable clue that the victim is in charge.

"It's important for you to see now that your whole family is not hurting. In fact, this is one of the best times for them. Harry and Brenda are finally getting along. Margaret is doing well. When your victim child comes out, what is your payoff?"

"I'm not sure I understand," she replies in her adult voice.

"Your victim child gets to feel helpless, out of control - she's blaming her feelings on Harry and his feelings. They didn't make you feel this way. You are choosing to feel this way. By blaming and holding on to your feelings and gathering more hurts for ammunition, you are choosing to suffer - to allow the victim to control your sex life with your husband."

Carole responds, the victim quality now completely gone from her voice, "I didn't think I was blaming Harry."

"You weren't consciously blaming him, but you were subconsciously blaming him. Remember, the subconscious is 90% of your mind. You are also blaming Helen because subconsciously you associate her with his family, even though she didn't grow up with them - she's not even a blood relative."

"Take the pillow and talk to Harry now and tell him what you can forgive him for," I suggest.

"I don't know if I can ever forgive you for betraying me with Helen. It's all her fault that I can't feel passion for you anymore."

"Carole, as long as you continue to blame someone else for your feelings, you are giving them power in your life and you will continue to feel helpless."

"Well, how can I stop blaming them?" she asks.

"By taking responsibility for your feelings. Make some 'I' statements such as, 'I feel hurt and so I have chosen to shut off my feelings.' 'I have chosen to not trust you.' Talk to Harry now."

"I turned myself off to you when you betrayed me. I need to feel that I can trust you again."

"Good. Now, what will it take for you to trust him? Has he been faithful ever since this thing with Helen five years ago?" She nods yes. *What will it take? Five more years? Ten more? What? I wonder.*

"You have the switch, Carole. Only you can turn it on or off, take back control and stop playing the helpless victim."

Carole replies, "But I'm so afraid of being hurt."

"Who is hurting you now? Perhaps Harry hurt you five years ago, but you are hurting yourself now by cutting off your passion. You're the one depriving yourself of intimacy with your husband. Talk to Harry now."

"I don't know what to say. I'm too ashamed because I'm hurting our relationship because I can't let go."

"Take responsibility for yourself and say, 'I won't let go'."

"I won't let go."

"Okay, now be Harry and respond."

46

"I don't understand why you won't let go. I've tried everything I know to show you how much I love you and how much you mean to me. I'm so sorry I've hurt you."

"Okay, Carole, respond to Harry now and tell him what it will take for you to let go."

Still feeling somewhat confused, but certainly moving out of the victim role, Carole states, "I don't know what it will take for me to be able to let go."

"What it takes is for you to choose not to be the victim any longer. You have begun to take responsibility for your feelings. Now you must choose to no longer want to suffer or be helpless, or blame others. You must be able to forgive, let go and open up. Talk to Harry now."

All of a sudden, Carole has a new tone in her voice as she responds, "I want to be in control. I don't want to hurt anymore."

"Good, now talk to the victim part of you."

"I don't want to hurt or suffer or feel guilty anymore. I want to be strong and in control. I don't want to feel hurt. I want to get rid of the things that cause me pain. I want to forgive Harry and even Helen, if that's what it takes. I want to let myself feel all the good things again."

"Good! Now tell Harry directly what you are forgiving him for."

"I can forgive you for what happened with Helen and for other things that I felt you hurt me with. It doesn't matter anymore. What's important is how much we love each other; our marriage, our family and what we have together," she says in a much stronger voice.

Knowing this one will be difficult, I now instruct her to talk to Helen.

"It's not important anymore what you did to me. I'm not going to let you hurt me anymore. What's important is the life Harry and I have together now." Her voice is firm and strong, no sign of the victim anywhere.

"Okay, Carole, now talk to the part of you that has been closing off to Harry. Tell that part of you how you feel now. It's okay to open up to Harry. You know you can trust him now. He's shown you a million times how much he loves you. You know you're the most important thing in his life and he is in yours. You can stop punishing him and yourself now!"

I can feel the change-over from the victim to the winner now. She originally came in being upset because she had not been able to control her eating any longer. This is usually the case. When the helpless victim part of the personality takes over, it becomes obvious: the symptoms of being out of control spill over into eating, drugs or alcohol. So I instruct Carole to talk to herself about weight loss now.

"Carole, you want to be slim and healthy and to wear pretty clothes. You don't have to keep punishing yourself with food," she tells herself. Did you catch that? Right here in this statement is exactly how the victim operates. They guilt to control other people, but they also use it on themselves. The victim part of Carole had been making her feel guilty about not opening up to her husband sexually, and then punishing her by keeping her fat. When instructed properly, the subconscious mind will reveal exactly what it has been doing to the person.

I now feel that Carole has made the transition from victim position to winner. I complete the therapy session with reinforcement of what has occurred and positive affirmations. "You now are changing over from victim to winner, getting in touch with the healthy part of your adult personality. You are learning to build a new, healthy adult relationship with your husband using all your lessons from the past as your foundation."

Carole is ecstatic when she awakens from her session. She says she feels like a new person. She feels confident that she will be back on track with her eating program and she decides to begin using a rowing machine to help shed the extra pounds more quickly.

It has been interesting to see how Carole and Harry can both feel good and strong at the same time. They are learning to release the victim triangle in their family. They are reporting incredible improvement in their lives since completion of therapy.

The Persecutor Personality - Domination through Abuse

I would now like you to meet Terry and Marilyn. Terry has been in law enforcement for many years. Many people with persecutor-type personalities choose occupations where they can dominate, persecute and control others and get paid for it; law enforcement is one of those professions. I do not, of course, mean to say that all law enforcement people are persecutors. Persecutors can be found in all walks of life.

In his younger days as a deputy, Terry was pretty macho. He had that strong, unyielding type of character that you can always recognize as a persecutor, and he was always on a "campaign." That's another sure sign of the persecutor. They are often "out to get someone." Terry was out to get "those child molesters" or "those damn dopers." He was usually on a "mission" of one sort or another.

All this was the front you would see if you knew Terry down at the Sheriff's office. If you knew Terry on a personal basis, however, you

48

might know that underneath all this bravado was a victim child who felt helpless. Terry was a victim to his dependency on women. His mother was the suffering martyr, who controlled him through guilt. She kept him dependently tied to her most of his adult life.

Terry learned the game, of course, from his father. As a child, Terry and his mother were victims of his domineering, critical and sometimes abusive father. They had to walk around on eggshells to prevent his persecutions. Terry often tried to be the rescuer of his mom, but ended up feeling like the victim when his dad would turn on him. As much as he hated his dad, Terry began to take on his role, that of the persecutor. As a child, he was "the Bully" in school; as he got older, "Mr. Self-righteous."

Because of his "macho role," victim women are always attracted to Terry. They think he's strong, someone they can depend on. And, not surprisingly, victim women give Terry a *raison d'être*. His mission: "to rescue" just as he had tried to do with his mother. The problem is that he usually turns his persecuting personality on those same women he started out trying to rescue.

When I first met Terry and Marilyn, they were heavily involved in the victim triangle. Their entire relationship was a classic example. Terry had been devastated by his first divorce and was feeling persecuted by his ex-wife. He was down and out with nowhere to go. Enter Marilyn, the Rescuer. She picked him up as you would a stray puppy, took him home and gave him love. She fed him, clothed him, and gave him a place to stay. She spent her days searching for an apartment for Terry. Remember, rescuers need to be needed and Marilyn was in her glory! She was his female knight in shining armor.

Their love affair lasted until they got married. All of a sudden, Marilyn's "mission" was over and her *raison d'être* was gone. This is when the roles began to shift. Marilyn changed from rescuer to victim, since she felt Terry no longer needed her. He worked long hours and was gone many evenings. She began to withdraw and Terry, feeling abandoned, began to issue demands. The more abandoned he felt, the more noticeable was the switch to the role of persecutor. As he began to persecute her, she no longer felt like being vulnerable with him in the bedroom so the sex was no longer there; Marilyn was not the same as she was when she was rescuing him. He didn't understand; he only reacted by trying to "make Marilyn give him back the love they had." The more he demanded, the more she withdrew. He then began to take out his anger on her children. He discovered them smoking pot, and being a deputy, used his authority to threaten and persecute them. This, of course, "pushed"

Marilyn into the victim role; she felt victimized by Terry, and she had to rescue her children from him! And so the game continues without end.

The important clue here is to realize that underneath the persecutor's "tough" exterior is a victim. And underneath the rescuer's "got-it-all-together" exterior is a victim. These roles are an attempt to gain a feeling of strength from the other person's weakness. This is essential in understanding this whole syndrome. Each person is symbiotically feeding off of the weakness of others.

So as Terry is feeling victimized by Marilyn's withdrawal of affection, he looks for strength by persecuting her sons. He begins by emotional abuse consisting of "put-downs." Not just put-downs but long tirades of put-downs. "You no-good lazy s.o.b., all you can do is sit around and get stoned all day!" Etc., etc., etc. These tirades would go on for hours until everyone in the house was filled with tension. As the tension mounted, it became obvious that someone was going to "snap."

Here is the point where the emotional abuse turns into physical abuse. Whoever reacted would then become the victim. If the boy reacted, he might get hit; if Marilyn jumped in to rescue her son, she would then become the target of the abuse. This is the only way Terry knew how to try to escape from his overwhelming feeling of weakness and being out of control.

There are so many families where these *Victim, Rescuer, Persecutor* games go on over and over again. They then become deeply ingrained in the subconscious mind of the children. Because the subconscious mind works in pictures and through repetition, the child begins to re-enact these scenes in school and with peers. The child may choose any one of the three roles to identify with.

The child in the family may choose the most obvious of the roles, the victim. He or she will then come home talking about being "picked on." You may hear things like, "Nobody likes me at school," or "The teacher always makes fun of me." This is accompanied by a long face, a "poor-me" attitude and a whiny voice. Children are mirrors for us - they reflect and duplicate what they see around them. Many times, however, they exaggerate what they see in us.

If the child identifies with the persecutor in the family, he will come home talking about all the kids he beat up. You will get calls from the school or other parents referring to him as a bully. Or he may just persecute through endless teasing and put-downs of other children. This is the child who confuses strength with domination and control.

50

The child who identifies with the rescuer will come home bringing stray puppies and kitties. She will "feel sorry" for them and want to rescue the victims of the world. As she gets older, she may become the "neighborhood social worker," attempting to solve all the problems of the other kids. This is the child who most obviously confuses love with pity.

Let's go back to Terry and Marilyn. Before Terry was born, his mother had a child who died. She became pregnant with Terry in hopes of replacing that child. Of course, deceased children are put on such a pedestal that no human being could ever live up to their greatness. And so it was with Terry, constantly trying to live up to his deceased brother's image.

Needless to say, this was something he could never accomplish. It put him into the role of "always having to earn love," an extremely insecure way to go through life.

Day after day Terry felt his mother continuously mourning the loss of her son. Being the martyr that she was, she would not let go of her pain and suffering. In fact, this is the *raison d'être* for martyrs - subconsciously she saw her purpose in life as suffering.

As a young child, Terry concluded that the way to get his mother's love was through pity and pain. The subconscious mind came to the conclusion that somehow love and pain and suffering were connected since he was sure his mother loved his brother. So he set about to create situations in which he could get his mother's love through sympathy.

Terry soon learned how to push his father's buttons to the point that his father would beat him. He was then, of course, placing himself in the role of the victim. The more he hurt, the more likely his mother was to feel sorry for him and rescue him. To Terry, this was the only way he could receive a "demonstration" of his mother's love. He had never learned healthy ways of giving and receiving love and this was all he knew. Terry carried this pattern into his adult life by somehow making himself "lovable" through pity. He found his first wife in bed with his best friend and immediately ran to Marilyn, at that time a friend, for love/pity. He was in deep pain and he called someone he instinctively knew was a rescuer.

Marilyn took charge of the situation. She put Terry up at a motel, checked in on him almost hourly and brought him food. She was there for him 100%, or so it seemed. In his words, "she put me back together." This is the clue statement that describes the victim-rescuer relationship beginning to formulate.

51

She began giving him love, all the love that he was not getting from his first wife. In her mind, Marilyn was comparing herself to his first wife, and giving Terry what he needed. This fulfilled her rescue fantasy. This is the "reverse Cinderella" where Terry is Cinderella who has been abused by his "wicked stepmother" (his wife), and is rescued by his "Prince Charming" (Marilyn).

This fulfills Terry's fantasy of getting his mother's love through suffering and pain. In fact, it further reinforces that fixed idea in his subconscious mind. He learns that the only way he can get love from Marilyn is to be in pain. These familiar roles are then labeled "love" and Terry and Marilyn get married.

From Terry's perception, the love-making was fantastic until they got married. This was a mystery to him until he began to understand the victim triangle.

Once Marilyn was no longer needed to rescue Terry, she turned off to him; her excitement came from her fantasy rather than from any "real chemistry" between them. This immediately threw Terry into the familiar position of feeling rejected and having to earn love. The harder he tried, the more Marilyn closed up. Terry then jumped to the persecutor position, thinking (not consciously) that he could dominate, humiliate, and intimidate as a way of gaining power and control.

This pushes Marilyn into the victim position since she definitely feels victimized by Terry's strong-arm techniques of trying to get love.

The next events are very interesting. It is amazing when you begin to realize that people are like giant magnets, attracting whatever they subconsciously need at the time.

Remember, Marilyn has now "switched" into the victim frame of mind since her rescuing is no longer needed. Marilyn is then attacked and raped by a stranger. She has "attracted" a true victimization. This is not to say that she wanted it or brought it on herself. But the way the universe seems to draw victim and persecutor together in situations is quite uncanny. Wearing the appropriate sweatshirt ("I am a victim") identifies them to others. Obviously, this draws Terry into the rescuer role and he refrains from persecuting Marilyn for a while. He can now, however, turn his persecuting side onto the rapist. And he does so with all the hate and vengeance you can imagine.

Marilyn goes through therapy and deals with the trauma of the rape. She uses the rape as another reason for not wanting to have sex. Terry tries to be understanding; however, he is still feeling rejected by her lack of affection. Slowly but surely, Terry begins his "pressure techniques" of wanting his way, which is more closeness, more love and more sex. The persecutor is beginning to show his ugly head at home again. The way to stop the persecutor is to get him back into the rescuer position. Then Marilyn has an automobile accident. Amazing, how we seem to "attract" that which we subconsciously need at the time!

So here we go again. Marilyn is again the victim, Terry gets to rescue her as well as persecute the other driver, and the vicious cycle continues. Marilyn gets to have another reason to not have sex and she also turns Terry's pressure into nurturing. Remember, the only way Terry ever learned to show love was when someone was in pain. So this situation allows him to express caring feelings which are otherwise absent. Here are two people who have not learned any healthy expression of love. They have been creating and/or attracting exactly what their subconscious psychologies have been familiar with - that love and pain go together.

If this sounds like a soap opera, I agree. In fact, families who are taught the victim game are excellent sources of material for such shows. The similarities between soap operas and victim families are extremely interesting. All the characters are very familiar with their roles, which are clearly defined and quite predictable. The drama keeps everyone interested since it is continuous, and always moving at a fast pace. Many people become addicted to "soaps" the same way they become addicted to "psychological games." They seem to fill voids in their otherwise seemingly boring lives; they are addicted to the *drama.* They confuse drama with intimacy. In fact, it is the continual drama which prevents true intimacy.

It is exactly the "addictive nature" of these destructive relationships that keeps the players coming back for more. After watching people hurting and in pain for most of their lives, one wonders why they stay together. Usually it's because of the addiction. This addictive quality is examined in Robin Norwood's book *Women Who Love Too Much.* The book speaks as if this were only the phenomenon of women. It is important to recognize the role that men play in this process. If a couple chooses to get divorced, it is not long before each one has the whole game going again. Often they will say, "I was very careful not to choose someone like my first wife (or husband)." The problem is that unless they are aware of the victim syndrome, they are only looking for someone who is *superficially* different. Victim game players come in all different shapes, sizes, colors and professions: don't be fooled by the packaging.

Take time with the questionnaire on the following page to learn how you can eliminate the stress of rescuing from your life.

BREAKING FREE FROM THE VICTIM PATTERN:
Eliminating Stressful Rescuing Patterns

1. List what your *needs* are, <u>emotional</u> and <u>physical</u>:

a.	a.
b.	b.
c.	c.
d.	d.
e.	e.

2.Whose needs have you been taking care of *instead of your own*?

a.

b.

c.

3. Are you aware of holding onto resentment when you do that? Y/N (Circle)

4. Do you subtly or not so subtly persecute the people you rescue with guilt, blame, criticism or rejection? Describe

5. Are you now willing to take care of your own problems? Y/N (Circle)

6. Are you willing to allow others to be responsible for solving or not solving their own problems? Y/N (Circle)

7. Are you willing to establish clear boundaries? Y/N (Circle)

Chapter 6
The Addictive / Alcoholic Family

> If you participate in the triangle in *any position*, you will get to
> experience *all positions*.

The alcoholic family is a breeding ground for victims. In 99% of addicted
families, the victim triangle is as predictable as the sun coming up. Many
families have their own unique version of the game, but the basics are
always the same. Typically the game involves the father as the alcoholic
and the main victim. The mother is the rescuer (the enabler in alcoholic
language), always trying to rescue the father from his weakness; this makes
him feel even weaker. In response to the rescuer, the father then switches
from victim to persecutor. He begins to persecute the mother. This
persecution may be in the form of put-downs (emotional abuse),
humiliation, or physical abuse.

The mother is then thrown into the victim role by this abuse, which
draws the children into the game. Watching their mother being persecuted
and abused, the children feel sorry for her (again the confusion of love with
pity) and, of course, are dragged into the rescuer role. This is an extremely
heavy burden for children to feel; their mother is in danger and since the
father is the perpetrator, they are the only ones she has to depend upon.
It's this exact situation that causes otherwise healthy, intelligent, normal
children to grow up into insecure, neurotic adults. This is why a growing
number of people in therapy are discovering that their problems stem back
to being an adult child of an alcoholic.

The game continues. Sometimes the mother will then try to defend
herself by jumping into the persecutor role. She may persecute the father
or the children or both. The children often become "pawns" in the battles
between the parents. Let's take a look at the story of Marty.

The Case of Marty

Marty came in because she was having difficulty losing weight and
keeping it off. She felt like there was some part of her that kept defeating
her. Marty is a very attractive, vivacious blond with a wonderful sense of
humor. If you knew her, you would think she was the last person on earth

to be a victim. Outwardly, she appears to be assertive, self-assured and happy-go-lucky. Nothing could be further from the truth.

As she begins to take off her mask, she reveals someone who uses all these facades to hide depression, low self-esteem, and a feeling of helplessness when it comes to her weight. She has a pervasive need for approval which is reinforced every time she gets a laugh. Her sense of humor, although delightful, is her biggest cover-up.

Marty is a successful businesswoman. She came in stating, "Whenever things are going too well, I get very nervous. I am always waiting for the other shoe to drop." This is a typical reaction of people from victim/alcoholic families. "As soon as I seem to get something going," she explains, "the bottom seems to drop out. It's like I take one step forward and three steps backward. I find myself sitting up late at night drowning my sorrows in a bag of chocolate chips. It's a pretty lonesome place to be."

Marty has a great deal of difficulty when it comes to true intimacy, because the main form of intimacy in her family was fighting. Now, you may ask, what does intimacy have to do with fighting? Well, in victim families, the parents usually do not know how to show normal affection through hugging, kissing or saying, "I love you." They do not know how to show loving emotions or to communicate in a loving way. So the main means of close involvement is through fighting. This is a way of being intensely involved and of getting someone's undivided attention.

Marty remembers her childhood: many evenings sitting out on the big rock in the backyard, listening to her parents fight. Many nights she went to bed reading to try to put herself to sleep. She was attempting to shut out their words, but also to be her own "parent" since they were too involved in their war to read her a story. In hypnosis, the violent scenes of the constant battle at the dinner table return. The victim mother is in trouble for putting too much mustard in the potato salad. The persecuting father turns over the entire table. The children scream and cry. They run outside to "the Rock" and the evening battle has begun.

One night, her dad stabs her mother in the neck with a fork. There is blood and the children are hysterical and call the cops. It is in this moment that they become the *rescuers*. He is taken off to jail for the night, and mother then persecutes the children. "There was no need for you to call the cops; we could have handled it. Now we will have to pay money and it will be in the newspaper." She persecutes the children with guilt. So now they feel bad as if somehow this whole thing is their fault.

They then begin to feel like the victim and wonder to themselves, "But we were only trying to help you, what did we do wrong?"

What is the war about? In every victim family the basic underlying cause for the battle is two victims, each blaming their feelings of helplessness and inadequacy on the other. *Blame* is what the war is all about; who's fault it is. What is "it"? It can be anything.

In this family, both parents came from alcoholic families. So they both knew the games well. Goldie, the mother, had been married before to another alcoholic abuser who left her with their first child, Barbara. When Goldie met John he seemed so different than her first husband. They were courting when Goldie became pregnant with Marty. This forced John to marry her and so the victim game began. John, of course, felt like a victim because he was "trapped" into marriage, and Goldie felt like a victim because John "got her pregnant." Each blaming the other, each using guilt, and each feeling victimized, the perfect beginning to 39 years of victim games!

And out of this "perfect union," Marty was born. This was John's first child and "the apple of his eye." All the attention he gave his first born made Goldie angry and jealous. He seemed to care more about the baby than he did about her (taking the victim position) and he certainly did not care about her first daughter, Barbara, as much as he did about Marty. With this victim thinking, Goldie began carving out the role of "the Bad Guy" (persecutor) for Marty. Here she had barely entered the world, and her role was being established for her. This is how it works in victim families.

Marty was premature and had to remain in the hospital for the first four months of her life. Since Marty was "his baby," as defined by Goldie, John was assigned to visit her in the hospital. This, of course, increased the bonding between John and his new baby daughter. When Marty was old enough to come home, she didn't know her mother at all. Goldie naturally interpreted this as "rejection" and in turn rejected Marty. It is typical of the victim to interpret many things as rejection so that she can get into her comfortable role of suffering and self-pity.

So here this innocent baby is being told almost daily that she has rejected her mother and that she is "her father's baby." She feels immediate resentment from her mother because she gets more attention from the father. She is also beginning to feel resentment from both of them; as true victims, they are blaming her for having to get married in the first place!

In the beginning it is just a feeling. As Marty gets older, the words are repeated often, "If it weren't for you. . . ."

In the therapy sessions, Marty begins to be able to express her feelings. Never before did she make the connections between all these childhood experiences and difficulty controlling her eating. We will talk later about compulsive behavior.

Marty begins to talk to her father. "I resent hearing how much you did for us. What a burden we were to you. You made us feel guilty for existing! It wasn't my fault," she screams. "I didn't ask to be born and I certainly didn't ask to be born to you. Stop blaming your problems on me!"

She is talking heatedly to her father as if he were there. "No wonder I always feel guilty!" she shouts. The realization is overpowering. "Because you got mother pregnant with me, all your problems were somehow my fault! What an incredible guilt trip. The message you always gave us was that kids were a burden. Don't have kids, you used to say, they are nothing but trouble. What a sick thing to say to your own children! No wonder I've never wanted to have kids. Here I am at thirty-five, childless, and now I see why."

For the first time in her life, Marty was getting in touch with the anger of being made to feel guilty all of her life. She had been holding in all this rage by eating and trying to shove down the feelings. She also used her sense of humor to "laugh things off" rather than deal with the underlying rage. Actually, before therapy she really was not aware of any of these feelings; all she knew was that she could not seem to control her eating. She was using food the same way her father had used alcohol: to kill the pain.

Every one of the children in this family ended up with addiction problems as adults. The two daughters ended up very overweight with compulsive eating problems; the boys drank and used drugs. It was the only way they had ever learned to cope with the overwhelming feelings of guilt, anger and pain.

Marty's sister Barbara was the family rescuer. Being the oldest, she had always been given the responsibility of the younger children. On holidays, it was Barbara who continually tried to play the game of "Let's Pretend We Have a Happy Family." She would plan elaborate family get-togethers in hopes that somehow everyone would realize they did love each other and would live happily ever after. It never happened! In fact, what did happen was that the family played their usual game of victim/rescuer/persecutor - the only game they knew!

On Easter, Barbara invited everyone to her house for Easter dinner. Marty did not want to go because after several months of therapy, she was well aware of the game. She was, however, persuaded by Barbara through guilt, the all-purpose family tool that gets just about anyone to do anything. Marty, knowing the victim game well, talks of how she had to suffer to go to the Easter dinner. "My husband had been working for 36 hours straight and we hadn't seen each other for four days. But we made that long drive (the martyr tone in her voice) just to see the family and to make Barbara happy. And then Mother ruined everyone's Easter."

"Soon after we walked in, Mother began talking about how I never used to help with the dishes, and that tonight I was expected to do the dishes." The set-up for the evening game! Marty became defensive and in her mind began the battle. She said nothing out loud, but began defending herself mentally. "You crazy old witch, I've always done the dishes. You're the one who has never done anything. You've always treated us like slaves! We had to do everything so that you and Dad could argue and fight all night. We were never really allowed to be children, because you had so many damn kids that there was no end to the work. I've never done the dishes? You're nuts!"

By her first statement, the mother pushes Marty into the victim role by persecuting her. Marty feels victimized and responds mentally by persecuting her mother. The evening is already ruined and it hasn't even begun. After a few minutes, Marty is steaming and takes Barbara into the kitchen. She lets it all out on Barbara, blaming her for always trying to get the family together when she knows they all hate each other. Barbara is busily trying to calm Marty down in an effort to rescue the family from the ensuing and inevitable blow-up.

The mother can feel the heated discussion in the kitchen, and is impatient to get in and play the game she began. This part of the game is called "Let's You and She Fight." It gives an otherwise weak person the feeling of being powerful. She can sit back and watch the explosions that she has created. Mother goes in and begins by calling Marty the troublemaker, using the *blaming technique* to make it look like this fight was all Marty's fault. "You have always been a troublemaker, ever since you were a small child. Now Barbara has fixed a beautiful meal, why do you have to start something and ruin this for everybody?" Here comes the guilt trip.

By this time Marty is outraged and begins letting out some of her feelings to her mother. Dad, predictably, is drunk, and so he begins to chime in taking Marty's side against mother and "poor Barbara." The fiasco escalates, drawing in a brother who ends up rapping Marty on the head very hard, "big brother style." Marty then grabs her husband and pulls him out the door. "We're leaving," she shouts, "and don't ever expect us back again." Marty is stuttering with anger after driving 300 miles and immediately being thrown into the same old family game she left home at age 15 to escape. "Why do I keep taking the bait?" she wonders.

In therapy, Marty is now in touch with the anger she has for her mother. She can see now how her mother has been the martyr all these years, *suffering just to keep the family together.* Marty begins by talking to her mom. "Don't you ever wonder why all your kids have problems? Are you aware that all your kids hate you? Barbara and I eat ourselves to death to get away from the guilt and the pain. John is an alcoholic and beats his wife; he learned that from watching you and Daddy. Troy is a grown man and has never been able to have a relationship with a woman; he's a loner and always will be. Bill is a pot-head; he's lost in drugs. What a wonderful family you've raised," she says.

In gestalt therapy we often have the person take the other side in an attempt to gain understanding of other people's feelings. This is difficult for Marty to do since she is so angry at her mother.

Pretending to be her mother, Marty did hit on a key issue. "It wasn't my fault. I had no power at all. This was my second marriage and in those days that was a disgrace. I had to make it work. I also had seven kids and no way to support myself. I was trapped and I saw no way out. So I stayed for you and the others, so you would have a roof over your head and food on the table."

This is how the victim/martyr justifies the position of entrapment with no way out. Marty's mother did indeed feel helpless and probably believed she had no way out. Marty points out an alternative to her. "That's just an excuse. You know that grandma hated what was happening to us. She told you many times that we could come live with her until you found a job. She had money and was willing to help support us. You chose to suffer and play the martyr. I'm sorry you and Daddy ever married. You had children you couldn't love because you didn't love our father. Together you and he raised seven mixed up, sad and lonely people - just like you and Daddy."

Marty became very emotional now as she began to realize at a deep level just how damaging the victim/rescuer/persecutor roles are on everyone. She began to see that her mother, who claimed to be "rescuing" the children by staying with a drunk and abusive father, did more damage than good.

"Mom, Daddy not only abused you, he abused us. I know you have been denying that by putting your head in the sand like an ostrich. Remember the time Daddy hit Troy over the head with a crescent wrench? He had to go to the hospital and we had to lie about how it happened. And the time he slammed the hood of the car on John's head to teach him a lesson? There were more of those incidents than I'd like to remember. So don't tell me you were doing us a favor by staying. How in the world could you stand by and watch us be abused? I used to think we were adopted because I couldn't believe you'd treat your natural children that way."

As the reality of the situation hit Marty, she began to release more and more of her pent-up feelings, the same feelings that she had used to push down tons of food. She was so angry at her mother for "putting her head in the sand," and yet she had been practicing the same denial by using food.

The *coup d'grace* for Marty was the time her parents threatened each other with divorce and talk about splitting up the children. Again, Marty talks to her mother. "You always had a way of making me feel like nothing, as if I didn't exist. I was certain I had been adopted when you used to say, 'I am taking my children and leaving.' I knew I wasn't included in 'your' children. I felt so abandoned! The ship was sinking and no one was in charge. My own mother was going to leave with my brothers and sisters and leave me with this drunken maniac - my father! I wasn't even worth taking. I drowned my sorrows by sneaking chocolate bars up into my room. It's the same thing I do now with chocolate chips!"

Marty is beginning to realize that she never learned intimacy or closeness. She is the only client I've ever worked with that even after a year of therapy could not accept a hug from me. Regarding this issue, she says to her mother, "You raised us to fight. That was the only way we knew how to get attention from anyone. You never touched us except with knitting needles or the wooden spoon! I never saw you and Daddy show any affection to each other in any way. The only physical contact I saw was violence or anger."

Marty reveals that she had always felt like a victim. Because she used food to drown her sorrows, she was always chubby. "I was always being teased by the other children about how fat I was or because of the clothes I had to wear. Mom, you never paid attention to me except when I was a victim. The only way I ever got your concern was through pity. If someone else was making crap out of me, you would act as if you really cared what the person was doing to me. So I learned to think that pity was the highest form of love. How ridiculous!"

This "victim programming" is exactly what leads many children into being sexually abused. There are several key factors. The first is that the child is so deprived of any normal affection that her vulnerability surfaces when an abuser begins to show caring of any kind. Second, the child feels so alienated from his/her parents that telling the parents what happened is difficult. And, of course, the victim role is so familiar to these children that they feel right at home with it and seem to attract abusers. Remember, I am not blaming the child for her abuse. I am, however, recognizing the programming that set her up to be selected as easy prey.

This is exactly what happened to Marty. During hypnotherapy, she remembered the only person who gave her physical affection was her grandfather, himself an alcoholic. She began to vividly describe the "grooming process" which sexual offenders use to "court" young children. "He would hold me on his lap and just pour out love on me. It was like nothing I had ever experienced before. I was in heaven. He would take me out for ice cream; just me! I couldn't believe it. For the first time in my life I felt important, like someone cared. I was only eight and I started to have a 'crush' on my grandfather. No one seemed to notice because they were all so busy with their battles."

Then a sadness comes into her voice. "Now I see that I wasn't special at all - he just wanted to use me. He would take me on the bed to tickle. He would laugh and play. I never had so much fun in my life. Then he began tickling me on my chest and between my legs. It didn't feel right, but I wasn't about to stop him. I didn't want to lose the only real closeness I had ever had. He then started taking off my clothes when he tickled and putting his fingers inside of me. It was so humiliating and yet I knew I could never tell. I knew my mother would never believe me and if she did, she would say it was my fault."

Here again is the *blame*. Even at age eight, Marty knows the victim game so well that she knows she will be blamed for being the victim. So, continuing to feel even more helpless, she does nothing. Day after day, she allows herself to be humiliated and abused just as she has seen her mother do for years. She had no strong role models for breaking the victim cycle. This is referred to in psychology as *learned helplessness*[3], and it is one of the most difficult patterns to break.

It was after the sexual abuse began that Marty started gaining weight.

During hypnotherapy she can see a clear picture of herself at age nine. "I'm fat! No one else is, just me. I wanted to be ugly so that I didn't have to worry about boys. If they were anything like grandpa, I didn't want anything to do with them. This wasn't conscious, but it is quite obvious now. My mother began nagging me about my weight. She'd make desserts and everyone could have some except me. Here I was, being the victim again."

It is very common for children who have been sexually abused to gain weight. This is their way of pushing down those horrible feelings and making themselves unappealing to potential abusers. Once the subconscious mind has "solved a problem," such as gaining weight to not have to deal with the abuse, there is not much anyone can do to change that decision short of therapy. This is called the *secondary gain* of a dysfunctional behavior pattern. The subconscious is resistant to changing the behavior, because to do so would "undo" the solution that has seemingly worked so well for so long.

Marty did feel helpless about her weight, unaware that her subconscious mind had "solved a problem" for her. Her dad tried to rescue her by bringing her apples so she would have something else to eat when the other kids were having dessert. Her mother persecuted her about it and Marty felt more and more victimized. This is a powerful demonstration of how parents can unload a problem onto their children rather than face their own unacknowledged problems.

In hypnotherapy, Marty was able to get down to the part of her that had made that early decision, and then change it. The subconscious mind is just like a computer: whatever information has been put into it continues to operate until "the operator" changes it. In the subconscious mind where all the emotions are located, many "decisions" are made on this emotional level totally without our conscious participation. Hypnotherapy is really the most effective tool for helping the individual to go down to that subconscious emotional level to gain awareness of what "emotional decisions" have been made and then to change them.

In hypnotherapy, Marty was also able to see clearly how she had adopted the victim role which she had learned in her family. It was very clear to her how she had jumped from role to role around the triangle. In some situations she would become the rescuer, and in others the persecutor.

During the time that Marty was in therapy, her mother actually decided to leave her dad, after 30 plus years of marriage. The children were grown and apparently there was no longer any reason to stay. She chose the "victim" position to get her out. She played the poor, abused long-suffering martyr role. She went to a women's abuse shelter as if she had nowhere else to go. Shelters are designed for women who are in immediate danger by angry spouses and who have nowhere to go. Neither of these situations was true for Marty's mother. She had a good job and many relatives who would have taken her in. She was not in any immediate danger.

In the shelter, she grabbed onto the role of the *victimized* wife who had put up with abuse for all these years for the sake of the children. This martyr role was very comfortable to her, as she had played it all her life. The children had never wanted her to stay - in fact, they had begged her to leave many, many times. Victims become well skilled at justifying their victim position.

Marty's mother could have left from a position of strength, which many women do. She could have chosen to feel good about the fact that she could support herself with a well-paying job. She could have rented an apartment and just quietly moved out. Her husband was often away on business trips and she could have kept the location a secret until he adjusted to the idea. The interesting thing is that when we stop "feeling like a victim," people no longer victimize us. We all wear a sweatshirt that tells others how to treat us. Some say "Kick me," and others say "I'm worthy of respect."

Interestingly, when her mother finally left, Marty chose to persecute her. In fact, all the children took their "positions" around the triangle. Marty persecuted her mother for being such a "martyr." She also became the rescuer of her father. "The poor old man" was her favorite phrase to describe him. Her sister Barbara took the opposite tack. Since she was adopted by the dad, she had always played the victim about being left out by him. So Barbara "rescued" the mother and "persecuted" the old alcoholic father. Even after divorce, the roles continue. By now you can see just how entrenched the roles can be.

Chapter 7
The Victim Triangle and Domestic Violence

The victim triangle is a way that people who feel very helpless in their
lives attempt to feel like they are in control. The problem is that it's
like trying to get control of a roller-coaster ride.

In her book *Women Who Love Too Much,* Robin Norwood talks about how
women become addicted to pain, using it as a distraction like a drug. I
definitely agree that this is true; however, I see some other aspects of this
addiction. I think people who play the roles in the triangle become
addicted to that game; they become obsessed with playing. It's like having
an unfinished game of chess or monopoly - you want to keep playing to see
who is going to win. It's the same type of desire to achieve completion;
but because the triangle is a never-ending vicious cycle, completion never
exists. This is the reason for the obsessive nature of victim relationships.
There is that compulsion to win the game; the problem is that no one ever
does. In fact, in the victim game everyone loses.

Another reason for the addictive nature of this game is that victims
confuse love with pain. Because pain has been so much a part of their
"loving" relationships, they subconsciously believe that pain is love. This
is why they seem to be "addicted to pain." It can be emotional pain or
physical pain. In many cases victims turn their emotional pain into
physical pain through illness or accidents.

Anyone who has been involved with people in domestic violence
situations knows about this "addiction." For several years, I directed a
shelter for abused women and it was the most frustrating experience I have
ever had. The staff (the rescuers) would help the victims escape from their
husbands or boyfriends (the persecutors). We frequently took part in the
dangerous drama of hiding a woman and her children in secret locations.
We would get police escorts to retrieve belongings while the husband
hopefully was at work. I had men coming to my office with guns
demanding their wives and children back. We set up secret routes for the
children to get to school.

The frustrating part was that after all this energy put into hiding and
"escaping," the victim would almost invariably let the persecutor know
where she was. Often, she would be "sneaking" phone calls to him behind

the back of the staff. And, of course, after her black eye healed or she was released from the hospital, all too often she would go back to him.

What I didn't understand at the time was that soon after the persecution, the husband would switch to the rescuer position now that she was obviously a "victim in need." He would then become very conciliatory; he would maybe bring her flowers or candy or something to let her know how sorry he was. This is where love and pain combine. Not only do victims confuse love with pain, but they confuse love with pity. The only time they can show "love" or caring is when they feel pity; and this, of course, comes when the other person is in pain.

So the victim of domestic violence becomes addicted to the pain, knowing on some level that the "caring" will follow. It is precisely this set of circumstances that perpetuates domestic violence. Then the "helpers" (rescuers) end up feeling helpless and victimized themselves when the woman goes back to the abusing relationship. "We tried so hard to help her, and then she goes back to him," is the incredulous statement of many shelter workers.

The important part of this for counselors, therapists and other helpers is to recognize that if you participate in this triangle in *any position*, you will get to experience *all positions*. You become just as much a part of the whole drama as the "victim."

The Difference between Rescuing and Helping

There is a difference between rescuing and helping. The difference lies in who takes responsibility for the problem and the solution. When the solution for the problem comes from anyone other than the person who has the problem, it is a rescue - and it will invariably backfire on the rescuer. A therapist can help someone by doing therapy which allows the client to see her situation clearly and make conscious and educated choices. That is the difference between rescuing and helping. It's the same with friends; as soon as you try to solve their problems, you are not helping them at all. The reason goes back to the Triangle. As soon as you rescue or try to solve someone else's problem, you are putting them back into the role of the victim, where you have taken the power and they feel helpless again. You can count on being persecuted or blamed when things don't work out.

I would say that just as 99% of all alcoholic families play the "victim game," so it is in 99% of all the "abuse" situations.

Sandy came into my office with a neck brace after her boyfriend had given her a whiplash. She was in a lot of pain, physical as well as emotional. She was an extremely attractive, bright and articulate woman, not the type you'd expect to be involved with a man who beat her.

She began to describe the physical abuse. "It was like a dream, like it was happening to someone else. I feel so angry and so guilty at the same time. I feel like he was just waiting for an excuse to do it. I would physically remove myself when I felt his anger building; but this time I took the bait. His ex-wife left town for the same reason: to get away from him. He used to vent his anger on her." Her thoughts were coming quickly now and they were not always connected.

I tried to help her focus. "When did the abuse first begin?" I asked.

"About eight months ago. He blew up and lost his temper. I started keeping track; he couldn't stop once he got started. It was almost once per week. His divorce about a year ago threw him mentally. I guess I felt sorry for him. I thought I could help him through it and give him the love he needed to recover." She sort of chuckled to herself, knowing how ridiculous that "rescue attempt" sounded now.

"I talked to his ex-wife and she told me that this has been a pattern for Ralph all his life. She said his son does the same. When Ralph found out his ex-wife had talked to me, he went to her house with a loaded gun. That's when she moved. Ralph felt intimidated by me because I was successful. Also because I was educated. One time he said he was going to destroy me and I didn't know what he meant by that. I'm beginning to understand."

Here is the beginning of the victim triangle. Ralph is the victim, having fallen apart after a divorce, and Sandy is the rescuer. The problem is that her rescuing him does not make him feel strong, it reinforces his feelings of inferiority and helplessness.

He naturally then begins to persecute her. This, however, is only the beginning of a very destructive and complicated game that Sandy and Ralph create together. They are both still involved with past victim relationships which they bring in to persecute each other with. Also, they use each other to persecute past game players, as in Ralph pointing the gun at his ex-wife for talking to Sandy.

"He moved in to our home. He and his son came to blows. He lost a big contract at work. He began drinking a lot. I've never felt so much negativity from a person, and yet he could be so loving and gentle. We had a big fight because I wanted him to leave. There was a big scene. Then the next day he sent me twelve yellow roses saying 'I was only trying to protect [rescue] you.' I felt like I was losing myself, like I was going crazy. I needed to know I was okay, so I sought out a friend, Mike, and slept with him. This seems to be my way of getting my control back."

The victim triangle is a way that people who feel very helpless in their lives attempt to get control. The problem is that it's like trying to get control of a roller-coaster ride; the minute you think you have it together all of a sudden here you are looking down at a great big "dip." When Ralph moved in, Sandy felt out of control since it hadn't been a mutual decision. Because of her lack of assertiveness (which we'll discuss later) she allows other people to manipulate her and then feels resentful. So her way to get control back was to ask Ralph to leave. He perceived this as rejection (persecution) and in turn persecuted her physically. Since she could not retaliate physically, she used her greatest weapon, sex. She persecuted him by sleeping with someone else and then somehow letting him know.

This is when the physical assault began. "He uses sex to punish me," she stated. "He had been drinking and as soon as I got home, he cut me off and slept on the couch. I told him to leave. He pushed me down. I got up, and he pushed me down again. I slugged him on the side of the face. He said, 'Oh, so you want to see violence?' That's when he really began beating me. I tried to get away and he kept shoving me up against the wall; I felt my neck crack really badly. He dragged me down the hall by my hair and kept bouncing my head on the floor. I finally got away and ran out the back door to the neighbors."

"I felt so much shame and guilt at the emergency room. I had to tell the doctor what happened. I keep wondering why in the world I got involved with a guy like this." I asked her if she had ever been abused before in a relationship and she said yes, for ten years with a man named Glenn. I knew that this was no coincidence.

Now we begin a hypnotherapy session. I explain the victim triangle to her since one of the goals of therapy is for release from the addiction to playing these "games." The first feeling she gets in touch with is anger. She is talking to Ralph. "Why don't you just go away if you are so unhappy with me? Why do you stay here and torture me? What's wrong with me? Why are men always rejecting me? I try so hard to be good. I hate every minute of always trying to get their approval."

When I hear this, it is an instant clue that there is a pattern of rejection and striving for approval: that addictive pattern in *Women Who Love Too Much*. I help her to go back to the beginning of these feelings and she goes back to being a small child. She is talking to her father. "Why do you always do that to me? I just come up to hug you and you push me away.

68

You told me not to do that. I just wanted you to love me. I missed you when you were gone. I can tell you don't want to be here. Is there something wrong with me? I'm clean, my dress is pretty."

Sandy begins to cry as she reflects on this situation and the source of her relationship patterns with men. "I never did anything improper. I tried and tried but he never gave me any praise. It didn't matter what I did, I was never good enough for him." She then begins to generalize this feeling onto all men. "They're all like that. They're useless and you can never please them no matter what you do. I don't like men having power over me because if you love them, they will hurt you. I married my first husband to get away from my father. I was afraid no one else would marry me, so I grabbed the first offer I had. I married Bill, but he was so easy to control he was boring. I didn't like that either."

Because Bill would not struggle for control and play the familiar victim game, Sandy found him boring. One of the most tragic elements of the victim triangle is that people who are used to love hurting don't recognize true love when they have it.

So Sandy divorced Bill and began seeking out men who would engage in a power struggle with her. Sandy continues, now deeply emotional. "I feel like I've lost me or maybe never had me. It's like I don't have the right to defend myself. Sometimes I don't even know what I want. It's like I can't have preferences or opinions. I'm so afraid of him; he has tremendous power over me. I can't get angry because that makes him more violent. I can't fight back because I can never win physically. I'm glad I don't have a gun because that would be the only way I could equalize the power."

As she talks and cries I could sense her incredible feelings of helplessness in the victim situation: helpless to fight back, helpless to win, but most of all helpless to climb out of this victim trap she had been in most of her life. She was seeing clearly how Ralph had abused and humiliated her in much the same way her father had when she was a child. I began to realize now that emotionally Sandy was operating from this *child* part of her. I knew that therapeutically Sandy was going to have to allow that child part to mature. She was also going to have to get in touch with the strong *adult* part of her in order to begin making clear decisions, especially in regard to relationships. Also, the *parent* part of her was going to have to be changed from a *critical parent* to a *nurturing parent*.

According to Eric Berne, in *Games People Play*, there are three parts to the personality: the *parent*, the *adult* and the *child*. In the hypnotherapy work that I do, I have found this to be quite accurate. I have found that the most effective way to make the necessary changes in life-long, deep-seated patterns is through hypnotherapy. In the trance state one can deal directly with each part of the personality, each of these *ego states*.[4]

Many people, after reading self-help books, say "Okay, now I know what the problem is, but how do I fix it?" A healthy personality has a balanced blend of all three parts: a "nurturing parent" whose self-talk is filled with praise rather than criticism; a "wise adult" who can make intelligent and well-thought-out decisions; and a fun-loving creative "child" who can play and let go easily. A healthy relationship consists of two well-balanced people who relate on all three levels with each other.

At the end of the session Sandy states that she will never be able to go back to him. "There's a part of me that's gone. I'll never be the same. I keep seeing me crouched on the floor and him grabbing me by the hair and pulling me down the hallway. I'll never forget it." I want to believe her.

As the therapy continues, it is becoming more and more clear that Sandy has generalized her anger from her father to all men. She then continues to choose men who reject, victimize and persecute her. So from a sample of five men, she can feel even more certain of her conclusion that all men are the same, and that "love hurts." The human potential movement has taught us that whatever we believe, that is what we create in our realities. Here is an excellent example of this. Sandy believes that men are no good S.O.B.s who will hurt you if you love them. And that's exactly who she attracts and chooses, subconsciously.

In the hypnotherapy, Sandy goes back to age six and the images that have been locked up in her subconscious mind for thirty years. "I'm sitting at the table and Dad's at one end. Mom makes a real nice dinner and she is at the other end serving everyone. Dad looks mean and angry. He always looks like that. I'm scared of him. I sit there all tense inside, so afraid that I will do something to unleash his anger which I know is right near the surface. I'm afraid to talk, afraid not to eat everything even though I usually lose my appetite when he's there."

The scared little six-year-old voice now begins to be obvious. In hypnotherapy, that's a key to knowing that the person is reliving an experience rather than just remembering it. Sandy continues, "Daddy is starting to fight with Mommy. She's trying to explain but that only seems to make it worse. They're both getting upset. I'm supposed to eat my dinner and not supposed to cry. I can't help it 'cause I'm so scared of him. I don't want to be noticed - if I could only become invisible right now! All of a sudden Daddy just lifts up the table and everything crashes to the floor. We're all screaming, Daddy's chasing Mommy with a wooden spoon. My stomach is in knots and I run for my room and hide under the bed. I hope they never find me. I just want to die."

I ask her to talk about the conclusions the six-year-old has drawn from these scenes in her mind. "Men don't ever treat you nice. Men control and dictate what you're supposed to do and how you're supposed to act. They never praise you. They treat women shitty and it's their right to do that. If you talk back or say how you feel, it just makes things worse so it's better to just try to be nice and hope they don't notice you. I can't seem to change them in any way so I just have to live with it."

These conclusions drawn by the mind of a six-year-old occur in what we call the "adaptive child." These conclusions to "be good" and "not be noticed" are the basis for the lack of assertiveness that we see in many adults, men and women alike. It is a basic survival mechanism. The problem is that once these "decisions" have been made they continue to operate until they are identified and changed. So Sandy continued to allow men to dominate and control her all of her life because her six-year-old had concluded that it was not safe to stand up for yourself or ask for what you wanted. This is why she didn't object when Ralph had decided to move in.

And it's her own lack of assertiveness that compels her to continue playing the victim game. When she sleeps with another man, it gives her some sense of power over Ralph.

Sandy further learned to fear men through her mother. As a child, whenever she did something wrong, she heard "Just wait until your father gets home. You're really going to get it." Sandy's response to her mother when using this tactic is, "I wish you'd just punish me yourself and get it over with. All day long I have a knot in my stomach waiting for him to whip me with that marine belt. I'm so scared - I live in fear of him coming home. Just get it over with."

In the domestic violence literature it is well known that women will often be aware of the tension building that leads to an abuse situation. The anxiety becomes so strong that they will often do something (not always consciously) to evoke the abuse just to "get it over with." You can see how Sandy was set up for this by the game ("Wait Till Your Father Gets Home") that her mother and father played when she was a child.

Not only does Sandy have stereotypes of how men are in her subconscious, but she has stereotypes of how a woman (herself) is supposed to be. "I don't know anything. Women aren't supposed to know anything. Women are only supposed to know what goes on in the house. If you try to show that you know something, you will get laughed at.

You'll really show your ignorance, so just don't say anything. Men are way up there and I'm way down here."

She now begins to reflect on her mother as she becomes aware of where these attitudes were learned. "My mother tells me she doesn't like it either. She says that's just the way things are and there's nothing anyone can really do about it. Men don't care whether or not you have brains. She's so unhappy, she's so angry. She resents it and hates it and yet she puts up with it. It's so confusing. She resents me too. I'm just another problem to her. She's always pushing me aside. As I look back I can see she is a giant martyr. 'Look how I suffer; this is my lot in life. I carry this heavy burden around and everyone else is going to pay'."

"I watched my father hurt her physically and emotionally. I kept asking, why don't we leave? I begged her to leave. Her reply was always the same. 'I can't because of you children.' I think she thought we should admire her for how she suffered for us. How ridiculous. We were all in pain. What's so noble about that?"

Many people live their lives believing that they must suffer. It is part of the Judeo-Christian ethic that somehow there is nobility in suffering. It seems as if many people are modeling their lives after Christ, who suffered. The Bible does say that he suffered so that we don't have to; he suffered for us. We do not have to suffer and we will not get to heaven any faster if we do.

Sandy now is getting in touch with the fact that on a deep level, she has a feeling of not wanting to live. She has never consciously been aware of this feeling. But with hypnotherapy she is able to discover that living with abusive men is a way of subconsciously "killing herself."

"I've always had the feeling that I just wasn't worth anything." She is now talking to her mother in the session. "I've always felt that I was just in the way, just another problem for you and Daddy to have to deal with. There's a big part of me that just wanted to die - to evaporate - just crawl away and die."

She continues, very emotional at this point. "As a teenager, there was so much tension I just couldn't handle it. I allowed myself to cease. I took some pills and ended up in the hospital. But even with this they continued to play their games! My father blamed it on my mother saying it was all her fault. Can you imagine how that made me feel? It made me feel sorry that I hadn't succeeded!"

"I keep feeling like I don't have any substance. I live inside this shell," she continues. "I'm not like the rest of you; I'm not sure what I like and what I don't like. I've just been trained to pick up cues from everyone else around me. I'm like a chameleon - anything to conform." As she gets more clearly in touch with this part of herself, what we call the adaptive child, she also remembers another part of herself.

"What happened to that 'spunky' part of me? I was awfully outspoken. Spunky knew who she was and what she wanted. My parents didn't like that part of me. In order to get their love, I had to conform. I was so desperate for their love, I suffocated Spunky. That's who I was killing when I took those pills."

"Spunky, you were too enthusiastic, too bouncy, too full of life! You were noisy, full of pep and you had a mischievous twinkle in your eye," she bemuses as she talks to that lost part of herself. She talks to Spunky as if to a long lost friend.

I ask her to recall any messages she received that told her it was not okay for Spunky to stay around. She goes back to a time when she was age six. Her mother is saying to her, "The way you jump around, no one will like you. You're always acting so silly, they'll come and lock you up. They'll put you in a straight jacket and never let you out. They'll throw away the key. Act the way you're supposed to. No one will ever want you that way. Act like a lady."

"That scared me. Whenever Spunky comes out now, I feel foolish and embarrassed. Yet, I can see now that she is a beautiful spontaneous part of me. After Mama began scaring me by telling me 'they were coming to get me,' I began wearing my little 'Sandy shell.' I wear it so much of the time, I really don't know how to take it off."

Sandy began to realize that there was another part of her that she called *Elizabeth*. "Elizabeth is the quiet part of me. She is the natural balance for Spunky. She has a lot of quiet wisdom and artistic ability. They never really appreciated that part of me either. Actually, they really didn't see 'me' at all. Elizabeth has been frozen for a long time. I can see her standing there with all these little barriers around her."

During hypnotherapy it is shown beyond doubt that we all have many different parts of our personalities, many ego states. Children who have been abused in some way seem to have more parts; you can understand some of them from this session. The parts often develop for survival reasons. The different parts "split off" according to what is or isn't acceptable in the family or school.

Part of Sandy's healing process is to reunite with the healthy parts of her which existed before the abuse. The spontaneous creative child parts need to be re-accepted back into her personality. I ask Sandy to have Spunky talk to Elizabeth.

"I need you. I know I can't go running through life, jumping up and down. I need you to mellow me out. But I do need you; I can't be happy unless I'm reunited with you. I can't be complete with only part of me going down the road. We compliment each other, like yin and yang. You have the freedom to move in your way, and I in mine. We can blend together, each finding our own rhythm. You don't have to be afraid of me, I won't overpower you. You have your creativity and I have mine."

Sandy now begins to cry out of joy. She is experiencing the reunification of her "disowned" parts.[5] Many of us as children disowned the parts of our personalities which were unacceptable to the adults around us. She is re-owning these parts of herself and beginning to see her own beauty, the natural beauty in these natural child parts of herself. This is the point at which self-esteem begins.

Spunky is talking to Elizabeth. "I love you. You are the elegance of me. You are the beautiful artist within me. I want you to rediscover all those beautiful gifts that got frozen way back there. We've been running around so disconnected. It's like we've been somebody else's version of the story. I want you to help me find out who we really are. We can do that by not repressing each other. You don't have to be afraid any more; I won't let anyone else hurt you. I want you to stop being a victim. You don't need to do that any more. Neither do I."

Here is a new subconscious decision to counteract the old one. This is what is required to change the old behavior. It is essential to change the decisions on the same level that they were made - the subconscious level, and in the same child ego state that they were originally made.[6]

Sandy then sees a big cage. "I'm putting my dad in that cage. He's all tied up, gagged and blindfolded. Mom is there too. You can't hurt me anymore. You can't see who I am, you never could. You can't tell me how to be or what to do. I'm proud of who I am now and it's you who are locked up, not me!" She chuckles to herself at the appropriateness of the vision that has come to her.

Sandy continues to come in for therapy and I can tell that the child parts of her are uniting and beginning to gain acceptance within her. She is becoming more assertive and definitely more spontaneous. She is beginning to develop her artistic talents and her creativity. She is beginning to like herself and to turn her energy toward developing herself rather than being obsessed with relationships.

Therapy is a process. It is a series of healing experiences followed by time and making changes. It is a process of incorporating the conscious and subconscious changes into new behavior. It is a process of discovering who you really are and shedding the "false selves"[7] you have adopted to survive in dysfunctional families. It is a process of releasing that overpowering need for external approval, and developing internal self-appreciation. And finally, therapy is a process of re-uniting with the disowned frozen child parts of ourselves, of reclaiming those disowned inner resources, so that we can begin to feel joy again – or maybe for the first time.

The Victim Triangle and Domestic Violence

Chapter 8
I Can't Stop . . .

Focusing on our fears is like viewing a cell under a microscope: they
become magnified far out of proportion.

Numerous people have told me that they think they have an "addictive
personality." No one really seems to know what that is exactly, but they
do know how it feels: helpless and out of control. Many people in our
society feel this way and the addictive habit is just a symptom. It is a
symptom of what is going on inside. I have worked with hundreds of
people who on the outside look as if they "have it all together." Perhaps
the only visible symptom is that they smoke, are overweight, drink too
much or use drugs. This is all you need to realize that inwardly this person
feels out of control.

When I talk about being out of control, I'm talking about emotions
inside which the person is using "the substance" to push down. People use
food, drugs, alcohol and tobacco as "pain killers" to push away emotions
that they don't know how to deal with. People use substances as a way to
deal with stress, boredom, loneliness, fear, guilt, pain, rejection, grief, self-
pity and just about any other trouble.

This compulsion can also be a behavior rather than a substance; for
example, a person may be "addicted" to sex or to unhealthy relationships,
to shopping or to gambling. Some people, bulimics, become addicted to
throwing up after every meal. These compulsive behaviors are really the
same as drugs, food or alcohol; they are used as a "pain killer" to numb
and run away from emotions that seem too difficult to handle.

Why do so many people have difficulty in dealing with emotions?
Emotions are part of the package which we are given at birth, one of the
"gifts" which make us different from animals. We are meant to learn how
to express our emotions "appropriately." I emphasize the word
appropriately because so many people allow their emotions to "take over"
their lives. Others use their emotions to harm other people or destroy
property. Others damage themselves by turning unexpressed feelings into
physical ailments.

To understand why so many people have a hard time expressing their
feelings, we must go back to our conditioning as children. Too often, we
do not allow children to express emotions and we don't teach them to

express emotions appropriately. We also selectively allow expression of emotions according to sexes. We allow girls to cry, but not boys. We teach our boys that they are "babies" if they cry, which makes them ashamed to feel sadness, hurt or remorse. We also teach them to repress fear. Girls can be sad, but not angry. We teach our children what they're not supposed to do, but we don't teach them what to do. How to repress their emotions, but not how to express them.

Children are extremely sensitive and perceptive. They are constantly searching for "clues" as to how they are supposed to be. By the first three years of life, their personalities are already formed and after that they are just continuing to adjust to their environment.[8] They will attentively listen to everything said about them in an effort to know how to win our love and approval.

Children are very adept at knowing what we expect of them and giving it to us. I'm not talking about when we say to them, "Now, Suzie, I expect you to clean up your room every day and make your bed." Suzie may pick up the very subtle "underneath expectation" that you don't actually think she is going to do it. That is the expectation that Suzie will respond to.

Parents are often oblivious to the expectations they have for their children, which they don't realize they are communicating either verbally or nonverbally. But the kids pick them all up. Expectations are very closely associated with fears. For example, a mother who dislikes her ex-husband fears that her son will turn out "just like his father." She begins to think she notices different characteristics in him and on some level these fears are communicated. The child picks up that Mom expects (fears) that he is going to be just like his dad. He begins subconsciously to "search out" information about his dad so he can fulfill his mother's prophecies.

Parents who have addictions feel helpless, and they fear and expect that their children will turn out the same way. Overweight mothers, who feel out of control with food, often nag their children about how much they are eating. The next day, however, the mother may use the child as an excuse to go get an ice cream cone, or may nag because she made a meal that the child doesn't eat. It is the feeling of helplessness here that causes the parent to react so inconsistently. She is grabbing at straws out of feeling panic inside.

The mother in this situation will be warning the child: "I don't want you to grow up to be fat like me." Those are the words that the child hears. But underneath, the child feels the expectation that that is exactly what mother thinks is going to happen. And, of course, the mother is highly engaged in teaching the child all the appropriate behavior to create an overweight compulsive individual.

The same is true in alcoholic families. When the child is young, the father may give him beer and think it is "cute" to watch him "get silly," or to calm him down. Then one day the child is eight or ten and the mother finds him drinking with his friends or she finds a "hidden" beer in his closet. Now she panics and yells at him, "You're going to grow up to be a drunk just like your dad." Instead of taking it as a warning, the child takes it exactly as he hears it: a command.

The more we focus on our fears, the more they become reality. It is like viewing a cell under a microscope: it looks enormous. And the same thing happens to fears as we continue to think about them and project them onto our children; they become magnified far out of proportion. Children pick up our fears and take them on as their own. Fears are learned just like almost everything else.

So in a family with a person who is addicted, all the habits may be taught, such as compulsive eating, drinking or smoking. But, more significantly, the victim feelings of helplessness and being out of control are taught. "Learned helplessness" is clinically one of the most difficult behavior patterns to break. And the ways of dealing with or not dealing with emotions are learned. The pattern is denial of emotions and then repression, using food, alcohol, drugs or tobacco to "push" the feelings down. When children are taught that they're "not supposed to feel," then they watch to see what the adults do to "get rid of" feelings.

Bulimic behavior is a telling example of what we have been talking about. Studies are showing now that "throwing up" is common among college girls as a means of weight control. This is alarming because it is so dangerous physically as well as emotionally. Physically, it can cause damage to heart, electrolyte balance, digestive system, teeth, hormone balance, and more. And in some cases it can even be fatal.

Psychologically, the bulimic is a classic victim. She feels totally out of control in nearly all areas of her life and quite helpless to change it. The compulsive binge-eating exemplifies a need to fill up a gnawing emptiness within herself. The compulsive throwing up represents a pitiful attempt at feeling in control. It also is a relief; regurgitating all the feelings she has been stuffing down with the food.

Many bulimics come from alcoholic families where there is continual emotional chaos. The alcoholic creates it and then uses the alcohol to run away from it. He uses the chaos he has created as an excuse to drink. The victim triangle abounds in the alcoholic family with the children feeling totally helpless to change things or to bring about any order.

Because it may be inappropriate for the children to drink, they begin to eat compulsively, especially sweet things like cookies and candy. These habit patterns continue until the child begins to realize that he/she may be getting overweight. This causes panic, and then the child discovers throwing up.

Another important factor, besides the control issue, in understanding the compulsiveness of bulimia, is perfectionism. This involves an all or nothing way of thinking that usually goes hand in hand with compulsive behavior. This type of thinking is taught in the family and may or may not be overt. It is "black or white" thinking. The dualities involve "success or failure," "good or bad," "starve or binge" – from one extreme to the other.

Bulimics (or other compulsive children) conclude that they are not lovable unless they live up to parental expectations. Often parents who feel unfulfilled in their own lives want to vicariously "live through" their own children. So they attempt to mold the children into all the fantasies that they had about themselves. This in turn causes very low self-esteem in their children.

Self-esteem in children is developed when children are respected for their own personal qualities, and when the parent allows the child to develop the unique interests and talents that he or she possesses. But if the love from the parent is conditional and is based on trying to fit the child into the mold that the parent has created, low self-esteem results. The reason is that the child never feels good enough, always insecure because she can sense on some level that it is not really her that the parent loves, but some image that she is supposed to create.

Many parents do not know how to love unconditionally. Their love is based on performance. In other words, if the child performs to the standards of the parents, then the love is forthcoming. If the child does not perform to the parents' expectations, he will feel stung by criticism and rejection.

This conditional love is the most devastating when it is paired with perfectionism. Perfectionism leads the parent to continually notice what the child has *not* done, or to point out the flaws and mistakes. For example, a child will come home with all A's and one B, and the parent will make the child feel bad for getting the B. Now the parent could have praised the child for the wonderful report card, but instead makes this above average student feel like a miserable failure because of the B.

Children raised in homes where there is at least one perfectionist parent often end up having a very low self-esteem and a great deal of inner tension and anxiety. The tension is caused by the fear of not ever being able to live up to being perfect, and therefore always feeling unloved. The perfectionist parent is constantly changing the rules and standards so that even if the child is able to reach one goal, the standard automatically goes up a notch. The child may also be compared to other children: "Why aren't you more like so and so? You know what a good student she is!"

I have known several young students who have committed suicide for exactly this reason. One young boy, Jason, was a top student, first string varsity football player, and on the student council. His father would constantly criticize him and tell him how he should be doing better, that he had such great potential if only he would "try harder." One night after an important football game, Jason was particularly upset. He had completed three touchdown passes...but made one fumble.

At home that night his dad completely ignored the completed passes and went into a tirade about the fumble. The next morning Jason was found in the basement where he had hanged himself.

Perfectionism is found in a great many alcoholic families because it has to do with insecure people trying desperately to gain some sort of order and control. They feel that if they can just get their children to be perfect, maybe they won't have to feel so guilty about the damage they know is being done.

Control is a major issue for the perfectionist person. It is also a major problem. Because they feel so out of control, they continue to try to control everything and everyone around them. They try to make themselves perfect, as well as their families. But their constant criticism and pointing out the negative has the opposite effect; people around them feel so inadequate that they stop trying altogether. They feel that no matter what they do, they can never live up to his standards or expectations. No matter what they do, they will never get his praise. So they quit trying.

The perfectionist also uses his all-or-nothing thinking to defeat himself. He is always waiting for "the perfect time" to quit the addiction. "I'll go on my diet next week." "I'll stop smoking when the price of cigarettes goes up to $4.00 a pack." Many times when they do start a diet, for example, if they "cheat" one time, they totally give up and start bingeing. All or nothing. I'm successful if I do it perfectly, and a total failure if I make even one mistake. They defeat themselves and end up feeling extremely helpless and out of control.

81

The bulimic is an interesting combination of all of these qualities. Control is a central issue for the bulimic. She quite often has a very controlling, domineering mother (or father) who is constantly attempting to control her life. The child usually becomes perfectionist by concluding that if she can be perfect, this parent will finally be satisfied and give her the love she craves.

The bulimic is almost always a high achiever, always striving to do better. She usually feels a great deal of underlying anxiety about performance because there is also the fear of never achieving enough. The bingeing and throwing up is a means of momentarily relieving the frightening panic. The problem is, the relief is fleeting and may in itself cause more panic after it's over when she realizes that she feels out of control again.

The bulimic also has an overwhelming fear, usually unrealistic, of being fat. Her fear gets blown out of proportion and becomes magnified in her eyes. She feels that if only she could be thin, which is equated with being perfect, she would be lovable. But she can never get thin enough and that's when the bulimia turns to anorexia (hardly eating at all).

As if the situation were not complicated enough, the victim consciousness is always there at the very core of the problem. The controlling parent of the bulimic usually is a victim, and that's the reason she feels so helpless and feels the need to control and make things perfect.

The bingeing and throwing up is a way for the child to tell her parent to "shove it." Because it is all done in secret, this is one area that the child will not allow the mother to dominate and control. In fact, the mother has no way to stop or control the child's eating habits. The child will not allow the mother to rescue her, and take away the only area in her life in which she feels any sense of personal power or control.

Chapter 9
The Victim Personality out of Control

Therapy is like peeling away layers of an artichoke; as you peel away
the outside leaves, another layer is there to deal with. And those leaves
can be prickly. After peeling away many layers, you get to the heart, to
the core of who you really are.

Most compulsive disorders involve the victim triangle. The nature of
compulsive disorders is that the person always feels "helpless" against the
compulsion. In other words, "the compulsion" has control of the person's
life. This can be any addiction including but not limited to alcohol, sugar,
drugs, gambling, spending, or eating. The compulsion becomes *the
persecutor* and the person becomes *the victim* of that substance or
behavior.

Obviously, since a substance does not have power of its own, the
victim is giving power to that substance, relinquishing power in order to
resume the familiar position of the victim. It is a well-accepted principle
that we humans seek out what is familiar, what is well-known. Actually,
after a recent horseback riding trip, I've realized that all animals seek to
return to the familiar. Have you ever noticed how horses don't really like
to leave their corral? They walk slowly away, yet they speed back in their
fastest gait when allowed to.

When children grow up feeling helpless to control their environment,
they tend to re-create that feeling. In effect they "return to the corral" as
soon as possible. The tendency to return to this "powerless" position is
increased when the child has observed one or more of her parents
continually feeling helpless or being victimized. We saw this in the case of
Sandy, where she recognized the source of her own pattern of being abused
when, as a child, she observed her mother being abused.

In the case of eating disorders, it's the food that becomes the
persecutor. The child is re-creating the "struggle to control" she had with
her parents by substituting food for the "controlling parent." Such children
are then in a continuing battle with food, always struggling to gain control
but always feeling helpless.

Rose came into my office telling me how bulimia had taken over her
life. She was totally out of control and was bingeing and throwing up at
least five times per day. She had been doing this for ten or fifteen years.

She was feeling panic. No one in her life had any idea that this was happening, since she had managed to keep it from her husband as well as her parents. Rose was living a double life and feeling like a victim of her bulimia. She described her terrifying fear of being fat; both of her parents were out of control with food and were themselves overweight. As a child she spent much of her life watching her mother's endless struggles with diets and fads to try to lose weight. Not surprisingly, she herself became out of control with food.

After the initial interview, I decide that it is time to begin the hypnotherapy.

I have Rose go back to the most recent time that she felt out of control with food. I have her get in touch with the feeling that seems to "trigger" her wanting to binge. She gets in touch with a feeling of emptiness. She's wandering around her kitchen feeling lonely and empty and then begins stuffing food down her throat. She doesn't even taste the food as it passes from her mouth to her stomach. On one hand she is trying to "fill up that emptiness" and yet as soon as she does feel "full," she begins to panic from the fear of getting fat. So she compulsively runs to the bathroom to get rid of it; leaving herself feeling empty again.

Now I'm speaking to the subconscious mind and asking it to go back to the beginning of this pattern of feeling empty and trying to use food to fill the emptiness. I ask her to raise her finger when she is there. Her finger raises and I ask for the age that comes to her.

"I'm a tiny infant. My mother doesn't really like me. She didn't really want another child so she leaves me with my grandmother a lot. My grandmother is rocking me but she's very angry with me because she thinks I should burp. She keeps hitting me on the back. It hurts. I can feel that she doesn't love me either. I can feel a knot in my stomach. I'm all tense and nervous. It's the same feeling when I throw up; it's like I'm trying to burp for her. It's also like I'm trying to throw up that knot in my stomach."

I ask her to go to the next situation that comes to her, and next she is four years old. "My mother is so mean to me. She always wants me to be perfect. 'You're so stupid,' she screams at me, 'why can't you do anything right? What's wrong with you?' She yells and screams at me. I can feel her dislike for me and it makes me feel that knot in my stomach. I feel so scared of her and at the same time there is this gnawing emptiness at the pit of my stomach. I eat to try to fill up that emptiness."

The next session Rose comes in stating that she felt much better after our last encounter. She was still bingeing and purging but not quite as much. "I was so much more aware of what I was doing. After my session, I felt calm for a couple of days. But then the panic returned."

I ask Rose to describe the feelings she was having. Her conscious mind has a difficult time with this description. So I put Rose into hypnosis and ask her subconscious mind. She begins to describe feeling helpless and out of control. "It's like the bulimia has control of me. It takes over my life and I have nothing to say about it. Then the panic sets in. The fear of being fat and the fear of being out of control."

I begin to tap her forehead, asking her subconscious mind to go to the beginning of this pattern. I can see that this is the victim syndrome where the core of the problem goes back to feeling "helpless and out of control." I ask her to go to the source of this pattern of feeling helpless concerning food.

Rose returns to age three and a birthday party. She is having fun, until her mother comes to the table to make all the little kids finish everything on their plates. "I feel so stuffed and now she wants me to eat more! She looks like this big monster to me, standing up there above us insisting that she made this cake for us and we have to eat it all. I feel stuffed!"

In the next scene, Rose finds her ten-year-old self coming home after school to an empty house. "My mother was always too busy for me. She never wanted me in the first place because I got in her way. She had things she wanted to do. I feel lonely and restless. I sit in front of the television and eat lots of food. Cookies and ice cream and sandwiches. I feel full, but I keep eating until she comes home. Then she starts making dinner."

Something about Rose's face looks uncomfortable. "What's wrong?" I ask her.

"It's dinner time and I'm full from everything I ate after school. I'm at the table and my mom is pushing me to eat. 'Eat! Keep eating! Eat everything on your plate! I came home to cook this for you and now I want you to eat it,' she would say over and over again."

"What are you feeling there?" I ask Rose.

"I feel totally helpless. She is so big and loud and forceful. I can't say anything because that would be 'talking back.' So I sit there and try to stuff the food in. I just want to be there with my dad. I want them to ask about my day. I want to tell them about school. But all my mother can say is 'Eat your broccoli.' She never wants to listen to me."

Rose pauses for a few moments and then continues. "It feels like there is this 'big force' over me and I am totally helpless to do anything about it. I'm so little. Every night at the table there is arguing. My dad and brother are yelling at each other. My mom is fighting with my sister. I ask them to stop. 'Let's talk about something else,' I beg. My mother stabs me with her fork! I cry and run to my room. My stomach is in a knot and I cry myself to sleep."

The "big force" that Rose is dredging up is her mother: dominating and controlling and yet underneath feeling very helpless to effect any changes in her family's unhappy lives. Rose is becoming aware of the tremendous pressure she feels to "be perfect." This is the only way she can, in her mind, win her parents' approval. So she continually tries to "read" what they want and then to become that.

It is becoming obvious to Rose that the pressure she is putting on herself is overwhelming. She was to keep up this front of perfection with her husband, her child, her family and her friends. The more pressure she feels, the more she binges and throws up. It is an endless, vicious cycle that leaves her feeling like a helpless victim. This is a feeling she has learned in her family and repeated all throughout her life.

People tend to re-create the same feelings that they had during their childhood. No matter how unpleasant the feelings are, they will be re-created just because they are familiar. Through therapy and awareness we can change these old familiar and unhealthy patterns. Now is the time to heal them.

The next session is a turning point for Rose. She comes in and states that she is feeling somewhat more in control, but she is still bingeing and purging. Not as much as before, however, which gives her the validation that we are on the right track.

I ask Rose to go back to the most recent time that she was feeling the urge to throw up and describe that feeling. She describes feeling scared of not doing what's right, of not pleasing others, and of not being perfect. I instruct the subconscious mind to go back to the source of this feeling.

Rose raises her finger and I ask her how old she is. She answers in a very small child's voice, "I'm little, about a year old. My mom is 'hovering' over me." She begins to get very upset. "She won't even let me try. She's there already thinking I can't do it. She's always doing it for me. I feel suffocated by her. I can't breathe with her hovering over me."

I instruct her to talk to her mother now, in this scene at age one, and tell her how she feels. "I feel choked by your constant hovering over me. I don't have any room to breathe. I don't have any room to be me. You're always there wanting me to be perfect, and yet thinking that I can't do things. You never give me the chance to learn. You're robbing me of the chance to learn. I feel so helpless to have control of my life with you always right there."

The things she is saying to her mother sound very familiar. These are the same feelings she has described about the bulimia. "How does this relate to your purging habit?" I ask her.

She begins to get excited. "It's the same - it's the same exact feeling!" she exclaims. Now we're getting down to the source of this problem. I instruct her to talk to her habit now. She begins, "You keep me from doing what I want. You are always there, hovering over me. I feel choked and suffocated by you. You always get in my way. You rob me of the chance to really be me. You make me feel totally out of control. I feel controlled by you. I feel squashed by you. You take hold of me and I can't get away from you. Leave me alone, get out of my life!" she yells.

Rose is beginning to realize that her habit is producing the same feelings inside of her that her mother had produced when she was growing up. She begins talking to her mother now. "I need the freedom to live my life without you always being there. I need to be free of your critical eye always watching over me. You're always thinking I'm doing it wrong. I feel so trapped by you. And now I've created a neurosis with food that I feel trapped by. I've re-created you in my life!" This is a very heavy realization for Rose. For a few moments, she is overwhelmed by it.

She continues since she is now in a very deep state of hypnosis, a state where the "truth" becomes painfully obvious. "I so much wanted to be perfect so you would love me. But nothing I did ever seemed to please you. I kept trying harder and harder and just felt more and more helpless. I felt like I was doing so much wrong I could never be perfect."

Rose begins to experience a time when she is a very small child. "I'm in diapers. Her eyes are staring at me. She's too close!" I can see that a kind of panic is setting in, the same type of panic feeling she describes when she has to throw up. She begins to scream at her mother now.

"You're too close, *back off*! Get out of my face. I've got to 'get rid' of you – you're smothering me. I'm choking. I feel like I have to throw up!"

She becomes overwhelmed with her truth now.

She is laughing and crying at the same time as her realization becomes so blatantly obvious. "That's it!" she shouts. "Every time I throw up, I'm trying to 'get rid' of my mother. I'm trying to 'get rid' of all those feelings inside of me. I'm throwing up that panic and fear that's sitting in my gut. And I'm re-creating this situation over and over again every day of my life. How sick!"

Rose is excited by her clear moment of "truth." She can see now how she was making herself into a victim, a victim of her addictive habit. Once the realization comes, that she has created this, the healing can take place. She then realizes that she is in control since she has created it. I can then instruct her to claim that power and use it to create healthy habits in her life.

I instruct Rose now to become the loving, nurturing parent to the little child within her. I ask her to *re-parent* her inner child. She begins to talk to the child within. "I love you just the way you are. I trust that you can do things by yourself. You don't have to be perfect because I love you unconditionally." There is a soft feeling in the room. Rose has her arms around herself and I can feel the love she has for her child within, for herself. Once she begins to know that she is lovable and that she deserves love, the healing takes place.

She continues to talk to her child. "I'm your new mom. I feel great and I think you're great! I believe that you make good choices. You have good judgment. You are very wise. I can love you without smothering you. I can love you and give you the space to be yourself." Rose begins to cry with joy now as she experiences true self-love on a profoundly deep level.

This is the beginning of self-esteem for Rose, a feeling she previously knew nothing about.

Therapy is like peeling away layers of an artichoke; as you peel away the outside leaves, another layer is there to deal with. And those leaves are prickly. After peeling away many layers, you get to the heart, to the core of who you really are. As Rose peeled away the first layer, which helped her to deal with her bulimic addiction, she began to take a really good look at what was underneath. She began to see the victim pattern.

Rose begins her next session, not talking about food, but about her relationship with her husband. There is an addictive nature to this relationship. She discloses that they have been "trying to decide" about a divorce for the past five years. Neither one of them is happy. However, neither one of them seems to be able to do anything to deal with the problem.

She explains that her husband, Tom, has lost his eye in an accident, and he blames her for it. This is the first clue that the victim triangle is in operation: someone who has been a victim blaming someone else for their predicament.

I asked her how he could possibly blame his accident on her. She told me that he was unhappy with the medical treatment which did not seem to be healing his eye. Rose did a little research and suggested some natural healing methods which he only followed haphazardly. When those didn't work, he blamed her.

Without yet realizing the pattern, Rose is now describing how she has spent her married life rescuing Tom. "I kind of hold him up. He's sort of just like a little kid. He doesn't know what he wants and he hasn't been able to find a job. I support us on my salary. I keep waiting for him to stand up on his own two feet."

So now it is becoming obvious that the husband is playing the victim and Rose has been the rescuer. Tom has created the victim situation concerning his work and has somehow "attracted" an "accident" where he can be helpless and blame it on someone else. Rose describes endless hours of reading to him and caring for him because of his eye.

I ask Rose what it was that originally attracted them to each other. She remembers "feeling sorry for him" because he was kind of the "black sheep" in his family. His mother never really liked him because he reminded her of his dad. She and his dad had been divorced since Tom was little. He had always felt rejected, and Rose's "rescue fantasy" was that she could be the one to love him.

After three months in hypnotherapy, Rose was in control of her eating disorder. After a year, she was healing the victim triangle in other areas of her life as well. She released her husband so that he could become responsible for himself, and she for herself. Rose's changes have been profound as she has taken full responsibility for her own life.

Spend a few moments with the questionnaire on the following page to identify your victim patterns.

BREAKING FREE FROM THE VICTIM PATTERN:
Identifying the Pattern

The most stressful area in my life is (assign a number from 1-4, 1 being the most stressful, 4 being the least, and describe briefly):

_____1. My home situation
_____2. My work situation
_____3. My family of origin
_____4. My body/health situation
_____5. Other_____

In the most stressful area of your life, take a look at victim/ rescuer/ persecutor patterns:

1. In what situation or with which person do you feel the most helpless or out of control (*victim*)?

2. Whose problems do you feel responsible to solve other than your own (*rescuer*)? Describe.

3. How or by whom do you feel persecuted, i.e., rejected, abused, ignored, guilt-tripped, humiliated/ embarrassed? Describe.

What *unhealthy* rules (spoken or unspoken) have kept you from dealing with this situation?

_____1. Don't speak about what is really happening here
_____2. Just pretend that everything is okay
_____3. Don't reveal (family/company) secrets
_____4. Don't trust your own perceptions

What addictions have you used to numb yourself?

1. Alcohol	5. Prescription pills
2. Marijuana	6. Tobacco
3. Cocaine	7. Food, sugar, caffeine
4. Sex	8. Spending money

Chapter 10
Addiction to the Game

> Families addicted to playing the Victim Game are like a vacuum cleaner: they try to suck everyone into their game. If you won't play, you are automatically cast into the role of "bad guy" or persecutor. If you do play, you will also end up in that role.

I'm going to introduce you to a family that is literally addicted to the victim game. They are addicted to "playing" the way some people are addicted to cocaine or alcohol; they can't seem to do without it. It's similar to the way many people are addicted to "soaps." They are addicted to the drama. It's as if they fear that without the "game" their lives would be unbearably boring. They bring to mind a line from the old Fleetwood Mac song *Dreams*: "Players only love you when they're playing." This family is like a vacuum cleaner; they suck everyone and everything into their game. If you won't play, you are automatically cast into the role of "the bad guy" or persecutor. If you do play, you will also end up in that role. No matter what, you always lose. This is the kind of game you want to avoid at all costs.

The theme of addictions runs all through victim families. In the Rift family everyone has some type of addiction. Both parents are addicted to alcohol and tobacco. The children are also addicted to tobacco and have gone through various battles with substance abuse. Another obvious addiction is that of unhealthy relationships.

I first met Toni when she came into my office because her life was falling apart. She kept attracting alcoholic men who could not give her what she needed. *Women Who Love Too Much* describes the addictive nature of Toni's relationships. Coming from a victim family, she felt helpless in her own life and attracted helpless men whom she attempted to rescue. The problem was that she herself was the one who needed rescuing. So she was continually disappointed when the men fell apart and she realized they couldn't help her and she couldn't help them. On some level she was aware of being a victim.

And here is her victim situation. Toni is now divorced from her alcoholic, abusive husband who does not pay child support. She has two small children and few job skills. So she goes on welfare and tries to maintain a decent life-style for her children. She has a few friends, all of whom are victims also. She usually plays the role of rescuer with them as they continue their own dramas of pain and suffering. She spends hours on the phone listening to "poor me" stories and attempting to help people who don't want anything but sympathy and someone with whom to play "Ain't it Awful."

Most of Toni's social life seems to revolve around her family and the games that they continue to play. Her mother, Betty, is an attractive but totally insecure woman. She was raised Catholic and cleverly uses guilt, fear and morality to control and manipulate those around her, including herself. Toni is heavily involved in attempting to rescue her mother from her dad, Cliff, who is cast into the role of the family "bad guy." Betty, of course, plays the victim who is always being persecuted by Cliff.

Cliff and Betty use their children as pawns in the continuing battle of their marriage. They are each attempting to prove that the other one is "wrong." Wrong about what? Anything and everything. Psychologically, they are both attempting to prove that they are the victim, deserving of pity (love), and the other person is the bad guy deserving of blame and scorn. The children are forced to take sides.

Betty has chosen Toni and Stuart to be on her side. She has trained them to be her rescuers. She also rescues Stuart from his dad, which sets up a battle between them. Cliff has been given Lisa, the youngest daughter, and Cliff Jr. since both of them are "more like him." So the lines are drawn, the stage is set for a continuing saga which never seems to end.

The drama-battle began very early in Betty and Cliff's relationship. They were teenagers, dating each other and supposedly in love. Cliff says that Betty went out with someone else, which deeply hurt his feelings and pushed his "rejection button." She says that it was he who first went out with someone else, causing her to feel rejected. Perhaps the answer to the metaphysical question of which came first will never be known. It's not really important at this point, since it certainly would not stop the drama-battle game.

Betty and Cliff had learned the victim game in their own families and found each other like a magnet finds metal. We are attracted to people in our lives for many reasons. One may be, as Shirley MacLaine contends, to work out past lives. Another, I believe, is that we are provided with relationships that give us the opportunity to heal or change the old unhealthy patterns of our past. Whether the past is other lives, or the recent past of our own families, is not the main issue. Through our relationships we must learn to love ourselves and others; it's that simple.

Just as in business the bottom line is money, in relationships the bottom line is love. Love seems to be so difficult for us and yet it is so

92

simple that children can do it better than we can as adults. Why do we take such a simple basic feeling and complicate it with pain and hurt and fear? We use it to manipulate others and control their lives. We use it as a tool and a weapon in the battlefields of our relationships. And what are all the battles about? About love! *Am I lovable? Do you love me? Do I love you? Do you love someone else?*

Instead of relationships being our battlegrounds, they must become our universities. Within the walls of these universities we learn what self-esteem is all about. We learn that to love ourselves is the opposite of being selfish. When we feel good inside, it is like having a well that is filled with love: we have so much more to give others. When there is self-hate and insecurity inside, that is all we have to give to others.

We get so focused on making someone else prove that they love us, all the while never being able to accept that we are lovable. So many people feel unworthy of love that they destroy relationship after relationship, unable to accept the love that is there. So loving ourselves is the key to successful relationships.

I have watched Cliff and Betty destroy their entire family over this issue; each one of them believing that they are not worthy of love, and so fighting to try to make the other one "prove" to them that they are. But since they themselves don't believe it, it can never be proven. "Why don't you love me?" is the constant cry. "I do love you," the continuing reply. "No you don't," she chides again. And it goes on and on.

In the University of Love and Relationships, we learn that we all create our reality by what we believe. So, if our main belief system tells us that we are unlovable, we become so unlovable that our belief becomes reality. And then at least we know we are "right." When becoming "right" becomes more important than being loved, we find ourselves in the brutal clutches of the victim triangle.

We teach people how to treat us by the verbal and non-verbal messages we give out, by the message on our sweatshirt: "Hurt me," or "Kick me" or "I'm unlovable." In this way, we do create our reality by what we believe. And this is why we must first believe that we are lovable before we can attract someone to love us.

There is a difference between attracting a rescuer and a lover. Remember, the victim/rescuer confuses love with pity. For example, when Betty was growing up she lived in a family where her mother was the victim and the dad was the "bad guy." He was a womanizer, and everyone felt sorry for "poor Mom." To a child, this pity looked like love. Mom felt sorry for herself and so taught the children how to create self-pity. Mom felt sorry for Betty and her sister because they didn't have a dad and this pity also felt like caring/love to the children.

Betty grew up creating situations where she could be the victim and emulate the self-pity she learned from her mother. She eventually created a marriage almost exactly like that of her mother's. Her underlying belief that men could not be trusted and were going to hurt her by being unfaithful, became reality. At age 54, she and Cliff separated after 37 years of torturing each other.

The sweatshirt Betty wore said, "Cheat on me." And she carried an intense jealousy, the legacy of her mother. It's as if Betty married for the sole purpose of exacting her mother's revenge on men. Growing up she felt her mother's pain, and on some level wanted to get back at her dad for causing the pain. She found Cliff, who fell in love with her at a young age.

Betty hurt Cliff very early in their relationship by going out with his best friend. This began the cycle of love/hurt. Cliff, of course, was devastated, and in order to protect himself, he went out with someone else. So Betty was able to conclude, "See, I knew men would cheat on me." And so she married him and they played the game unhappily ever after.

Every weekend of their married life, they would make love on Friday night and fight on Saturday. Saturday night they would go to their club to dance. Either one of them could start the game by dancing too close to someone else.

Then the other would retaliate and they were off. You'd think that they would have gotten bored after 37 years of playing the same game. However, every weekend they would become intensely involved in the "argument of the week" over who danced too close with whom.

One week Betty would be the innocent victim who was being falsely accused by Cliff, the persecutor. Then the next week the roles would reverse, just for variety, and Cliff would be the innocent victim. Other people would be drawn into the game as persecutors also. If Betty saw a woman who was friendly to Cliff, her jealousy turned into violent rage and all types of fantasies. She was sure the woman was after Cliff, and he, being a man, was too weak to resist the temptation.

The children were always being drawn into the game, so they learned their roles early on in life. Betty would play "Ain't it Awful" with Toni. This put Toni in the undesirable position of having to choose sides between her mother and her father. She was aligned with her mother and learned to take on the legacy of her grandmother's jealousy and negative beliefs about men. So she grew up feeling distant from her father and was made to feel guilty for loving him; after all, he was "the bad guy."

Toni's relationships reflected this conditioning and the underlying mistrust of men. They also reflected the huge conflict Toni was in with regard to men: mistrusting them while at the same time needing them. This is quite common in women. Because Toni was never allowed to love her dad fully, there was a huge emptiness inside of her; basically she wanted "her daddy." Most of Toni's relationships were with older men who drank, and could not meet her needs. The men she attracted, of course, were all victim/persecutors like her dad.

Toni had a relationship with a father figure named Jerry. He had a daughter about Toni's age who drank excessively. At the beginning of the relationship they fell in love and both felt very comfortable with each other. The reason for the comfort has to do with them both growing up with the same "game plan." Jerry's father was an alcoholic and his whole family, as in all alcoholic families, played the victim game well.

Jerry was extremely insecure about himself, which made him an excellent candidate for jealousy, Toni's family legacy. He was also insecure because Toni was so much younger, and his fear was that she would find someone more her own age. If Toni so much as looked at another man, the fight began. This was a game Toni knew backwards and forwards. She also had a fear of intimacy with men, so the fighting would insure that they would never get too close. Fighting was the main form of intimacy that Toni had learned as a child; and children learn by imitation.

"How can fighting be intimate?" you may wonder. If you take a look at it, when two people fight, they are intensely involved with each other. They are intensely communicating and nothing else has their attention at the moment. Yes, the contact is negative, but it is still contact. Some people have never learned to show positive loving feelings, so fighting is much more familiar. Also, as in the case of Toni, trusting means getting hurt, so fighting is a way to have intimate contact without the fear of being vulnerable and getting hurt.

I am certainly not advocating fighting as a means of achieving intimacy, just describing it. For many people, it has, sadly, become a way of life.

Toni became addicted to her relationship with Jerry. She couldn't live with him and she couldn't live without him. The fighting was intense, almost every night. Her children were beginning to have bad dreams, bed wetting and lower grades in school. The tension was getting to them, too. Toni was fighting with her kids, especially her older daughter who reminds her of herself.

She began to realize how destructive this relationship was for both her and her children. She decided to end the relationship, which proved easier said than done. She told Jerry it was over, but he would not accept it. Extremely perceptive, Jerry knew all about addictions: they are dependencies. He knew, on some level, that Toni was addicted to him, and he knew how needy she was, that she needed the sex as much as she needed the fighting. So when Toni tried to leave him, he would just become more loving. He would feed all her needs for sex and closeness. But as soon as he was comfortably back in her life, the fighting would begin again.

The addiction is to the victim game. As soon as Toni begins to take her power and attempts to step out of the victim game, she starts to feel scared, insecure and out of control. The victim game is her "comfort zone." We all have habitual patterns of response which are comfortable to us. Even though they do not serve us well, we repeat them because it is all that we know. When Toni steps out of her comfort zone, she panics as if she had just stepped off a cliff; she immediately grabs onto the first thing she can find that will pull her back to her safe place, which happens to be the victim position.

In her victim position of neediness, Toni has an incredible ability to attract other victims who are more than willing to "play" with her. The only way that she could seem to get away from Jerry was to find someone else. She is so addicted to the game that her life feels unbearably empty if she is not playing it. Knowing that Toni was in desperate need of a rescue, a "caring friend" introduced her to Mark. Even with Mark in the picture, however, prying herself loose from Jerry was like getting peanut butter off the roof of your mouth.

At first Mark seemed very nice. It was love at first sight and Toni felt she would finally be happy. For a few days, Toni was walking around on her own cloud nine. She then had to tell Jerry that she had indeed found someone else and that their relationship was truly over. Now she had three people in her game and the roles were clearly defined. She was the victim of Jerry's jealousy and hurt. He, of course, easily slipped into persecuting her and this time he felt totally justified. It was like an instant replay of the games her parents had played nearly every weekend of their married life.

Mark was new to Toni and Jerry's version of the game. He did, however, have a vast knowledge of this seemingly universal game and easily spoke the lines of the rescuer. As he listened to Jerry verbally abuse Toni, it subconsciously took him back to the roller-coaster ride in his childhood. He always felt that he had to rescue his mother from his

96

alcoholic father and so here he was watching old re-runs of his family movie!

After several weeks of intense drama, Toni finally got clear that she wanted Jerry out of her life, for the time being anyway. Once she was clear and no longer giving double messages, Jerry did exit the scene. But she soon discovered that Mark was an alcoholic also. Although Jerry drank a lot of beer, Mark was downing at least a fifth of vodka every night!

Adult children of alcoholics (ACOA) are taught in their childhood to deny reality, especially if this reality has to do with drinking. So even though Toni was well aware of the danger signals of someone who drinks that much on a daily basis and hides it as well, she chose to ignore it rather than confront it head on.

Mark began sleeping at Toni's house every night. It wasn't that he was sleeping with her, but rather crashing out drunk on her couch. He wasn't much of a lover because the alcohol wouldn't allow for that. She became the rescuer/persecutor. First she tried to help him stop drinking (rescuer), then when she failed, she would nag (persecutor). This made her feel like even more of a victim. Why did she always seem to attract this type of man?

Mark had a son named Steve who was very likable. Toni felt sorry for the child because Mark was so hard on him. It wasn't just discipline, but rather negative put-downs and destructive verbal and physical abuse. As Mark began spending more time at Toni's house, so did Steve. Pretty soon they were living there without any spoken agreement. Toni just allowed herself to be used.

Mark and Steve did very little around the house. Toni began to feel as if she had four kids rather than two. She was now being called to school when Steve got into trouble, and would lie to Mark so that he would not be abusive to his son. Again she was rescuing Steve, and in the process feeling more and more like a victim.

Because the sex was so bad, Toni began to long for Jerry. He may have been a drunken s.o.b., but at least he was a good lover. She brought Jerry back into the picture and the game was spiced up again. This triangle went on for years until Toni was finally able to break it off for good.

Through her therapy and her awareness of the victim game, Toni changed her self-concept. She went back to school, earned a degree, and began to take power in her life. She realized that she did not need a man to take care of her. She also began healing her relationship with her father.

Toni then attracted Ralph into her life. This was the first healthy relationship she had ever attracted. Ralph was not an alcoholic, but a secure and independent person. With much therapy work, Toni learned to express herself and to make her needs known. After several years of learning to communicate clearly, Toni and Ralph married. It is exciting to see the changes Toni has made after releasing the generations of victim patterns in her life.

Part II

Treatment:
Turning the Victim Triangle into a Circle of Power
through Personal Transformation

What is the Personal Transformation Process?

I am certain that as you read this book, one main question will be going through your mind: "How do I change these victim patterns in my life?" Once you become aware of the patterns, they may seem to be so pervasive that you feel overwhelmed at the prospect of changing them.

The good news is that they can be changed, and in the next chapters I will show you how.

Awareness is the most important aid to change. By reading this book, you have become aware of victim situations that exist in your life and in your family. As these concepts become more and more clear to you, you will be able to identify what needs to be changed. Perhaps by reading this book you are becoming aware of your addictions and how they render you helpless - and therefore a victim. Perhaps you have become aware that you confuse love with pity, and have spent much of your life attempting to elicit pity from those around you. Your awareness is the first step in making changes in your life.

The next important factor in changing your life is absolute dedication to the process of change. Millions of people read self-help books every day. They begin to recognize their problems and unhealthy patterns. For a short time they feel excited, because the light bulb of awareness is flashing brightly in their minds. But seldom does simply reading a book make any genuine or long-lasting changes in a person's life patterns. Their habits, reactions, and underlying beliefs are deeply entrenched. It would be like having a severely impacted tooth, and merely putting some Novocain into it, thinking that the problem is solved.

So when I talk about dedication to the process of change in your life, I mean absolute dedication. This must become the most important thing in your life, because it is really what your life is all about. If you are not healthy in your mind, body, or spirit, what else could be more important to you than healing yourself? If you are not in control of your life and your relationships are not working, then what could be a higher priority to spend energy and money on? Nothing! You deserve to reach your highest potential as a human being. The only way to achieve that is to pledge your dedication to yourself and your personal transformation process.

Many times it begins as a result of mid-life crisis, a time when you begin taking stock of just where your life is going. "Crisis" is not the best description of this time; I see it as "mid-life transformation." It may be set off by a divorce, loss of a job, or any other radical shift in your sense of security. It is a time when you know that there has to be more to life than what you have experienced so far. It is a realization that what you have been doing in your life isn't working, but at the same time you don't know where to go from here. The transformation process is borne out of a massive state of mental confusion, emotional pain and/or physical disease.

If this description fits you in any way, then it is time for you to consider dedicating yourself to transforming your life. The first step is to declare your intention to begin the transformation process. The second step is to realize that even though you may be in excruciating pain right now, you have hit bottom and the only way to go is up. If you're not in pain, but just vaguely dissatisfied, you may still have to go through pain, fear, or anger to get to the other side of the transformation and experience real joy. But it will be well worth it!

People who are vaguely dissatisfied usually use drugs, alcohol, tobacco, food, sex, or television to anesthetize themselves from the feeling of emptiness that underlies their life. When you begin your process, you must get the addictions and drugs out of your life or your efforts are useless. That may feel like an impossible task to you, so the next step is to find the appropriate transformational therapist or program to work with.

Finding the right therapist or program might seem difficult to you, since you don't know what you want, where you're going, or how to get there. I will share with you my techniques, the programs I am aware of, and what the process and outcome might look like. Then you will use visualization, affirmations, and the phone book to find your teacher or therapist.

Chapter 11
How Hypnosis Works in Treatment

Trying to change habits using the conscious mind is like calling in a
plumber to fix your electricity; it doesn't work.

First let me de-mystify hypnosis for those of you who have not had an
experience of hypnotherapy or any professional training in the field. There
are two parts of the mind: the conscious and the subconscious. The
conscious part, which thinks and analyzes, is only ten percent of the total
mind. When you are in most traditional counseling settings with a
psychologist, psychiatrist, marriage counselor, or mental health worker, the
conscious mind is basically what you are dealing with. Any type of "talk
therapy" uses the conscious mind to analyze, figure it all out, or
intellectualize the problem.

Many therapies focus on analyzing you and your problems to death. I
call this mental masturbation. You can be analyzed for years, once or
twice a week, and spend thousands of dollars only to see very little over-all
permanent change in the victim patterns. Talk therapies may improve your
awareness, but that is only the very first step in changing. Talk therapies
may, on the other hand, give you just enough tools to play your victim
games on a deeper level!

You also need to make certain that your therapist is not a rescuer.
Many people in the helping professions have themselves come from
codependent backgrounds. If they have not dealt with their own need to be
needed, they may be encouraging your dependency on a subconscious
level.

The subconscious mind is actually where the work needs to take place.
The subconscious mind has many functions, all of which are vital in
making changes. To begin with, the subconscious mind houses all the
memories. Everything that you have ever experienced, felt, heard,
smelled, tasted or dreamed is indelibly recorded in this part of your brain.
These earliest memories and experiences become very important when you
begin to uncover the origins of victim dynamics.

The subconscious mind also houses all the emotions and feelings. This
is another aspect of the victim which needs to be expressed and explored in
the therapy process. When you suppress your emotions the way most
victim/codependents do, it is crucial to learn to express them in a healthy

way. Hypnosis, by providing direct access to the subconscious mind, really helps people to know what they are feeling on a deep level. Most people are greatly surprised after their first hypnosis session at all the feelings they experienced and expressed.

The key to treatment of the victim syndrome is to learn what your feelings are and healthy ways to express them. If the therapist you choose is not herself or himself comfortable with the expression of emotions, then the therapy will only serve to help you in continuing to suppress and intellectualize your feelings. You should inquire about therapists and ask if they, themselves, have a method for keeping clear with their own emotions.

The subconscious mind also houses all the habit control centers of the brain. Most people, when they try to change habits, attempt to do so with "will power." Trying to change habits using the conscious mind is like calling in a plumber to fix your electricity; it doesn't work. This is important in the treatment of the victim syndrome, especially when working with compulsive/ addictive habits. Hypnosis is the most efficient tool that I have found in changing habits.

Also located in the subconscious mind are creativity and the ability to visualize or picture things. Most victims have some very traumatic pictures stored in their subconscious minds. And since the mind is like a computer, unless the stored information is changed, the same pictures tend to replay over and over again.

After much of the emotional release work has been accomplished, a technique called *reframing* can be used. This technique involves "seeing" the past differently. It may involve re-creating some of those pictures in a new way. Using the technique of reframing, we are literally re-programming the old computer data that no longer serves us. A good example is Sandy (Chapter 7), who learned to live inside a shell of pretense as a defense against the anxiety of living in her parents' home. Finally, in one of her hypnotherapy sessions, she was able to liberate the child within, and to envision putting her mom and dad in a big cage. They are tied up, gagged and blindfolded. "You can't hurt me anymore. You can't see who I am, you never could. You can't tell me how to be or what to do. I'm proud of who I am now and it's you who are locked up, not me!" Sandy's child is vividly experiencing the reframed childhood, replacing the old subconscious, self-defeating images with new healthy ones.

The subconscious mind also has control over all the involuntary bodily functions, such as blood pressure, healing broken bones, and local

102

anesthesia. This aspect of the mind can also be tapped for releasing alcohol, drug and food addictions.

The most amazing aspect of the subconscious mind is called *the power of suggestion*. The subconscious mind is willing and able to accept all types of suggestions. It is very important to understand this concept because victims are usually highly suggestible. The reason is that they have been taught to look outside of themselves for answers and approval rather than within. So they become accustomed to taking on suggestions from others, especially negative ones. They also become very good at giving themselves negative suggestions, using negative self-talk.

So the power of suggestion is really a double-edged sword. Through hypnosis and the use of the subconscious mind, victims can be made aware of the types of suggestions which are to their benefit and those which keep them trapped in the victim triangle. They then have choices, which give them back their personal power.

Some people say they are afraid of hypnosis because they don't want someone else controlling their mind. When you learn hypnosis and how the mind works, you are actually taking control of your own mind. It's when you remain ignorant of how the mind works that other people can indeed control you. So hypnosis puts you in control of yourself, which is one of the important aspects of treatment for the victim.

In most victim families the negative suggestions that are given daily affect the minds of everyone in the household. After listening to them over and over again, the victim begins to replay those tapes in his own head. So it may be you who gives yourself harmful suggestions, subconsciously.

In the healing work with victims, I make hypnosis tapes with positive affirmations on them. Repetition is the key to changing the old negative beliefs. Just as the old "victim tapes" have been played many thousands of times over and over again, so the new affirmations need to be repeated.

There are many old myths about hypnosis which must be dispelled right here and now. First of all it is not witchcraft, black magic or sorcery. Hypnosis is a very subtle shift from the conscious to the subconscious mind, and back. In fact, researchers say that most people go in and out of hypnosis (the subconscious mind) hundreds of times per day. So this is not something unfamiliar to you. When you are driving a car and staring at the road, reading a book, staring at a computer or television, or engrossed in creating something, you are most often in your subconscious mind.

We can all relate to that feeling of having "spaced out" for a few moments or longer. During that time we were in a very mild state of hypnosis. You will not be "asleep" as the old-time hypnotists used to say.

In hypnosis you will just be very relaxed and you will hear every word that is said to you. You will also remember all of your hypnotherapy session afterwards.

Because of the many aspects of hypnosis and the dynamics of the subconscious mind, I have repeatedly found hypnosis to be one of the most effective and long-lasting forms of treatment. It also goes much quicker than talk therapy and saves people time and money. Hypnotherapy is for people who want to make significant changes quickly and efficiently.

Age Regression

The subconscious mind, as I have said, is just like a computer. It is also like a VCR. It records and plays back everything that has ever happened to you. This is quite valuable in therapy when you want to know what you are dealing with as well as what needs to be changed. It's like putting together the missing pieces of a puzzle in order to see the whole picture.

An example is a woman I worked with named Vicki. She had been terribly sexually molested as a child and had very low self-esteem. We worked for months on this problem, attempting to help her take back power in her life and to release the victim patterns. She was making changes, but there was still something missing.

One day I was inspired to do an age regression all the way back to Vicki's earliest experience. I asked the subconscious mind to take us back to the source of her low self-esteem. Vicki paused for a long time and then stated she felt really little. It turned out that she regressed back to being in the womb. At first she felt warm and safe.

Suddenly she began sobbing. I asked her what was happening and she yelled, "They don't want me. My mother wants to get rid of me. She doesn't want a baby!" In an instant it all made sense. Vicki had low self-esteem because she felt unwanted even before her birth. She entered into the world feeling rejected and feeling like a victim from the beginning. No wonder she continued to attract persecutors and rescuers into her life.

The subconscious mind, through the age regression technique, was able to bring to consciousness the missing piece of the puzzle. It was very powerful and led Vicki to *reframe* that experience. She eventually was able to re-parent the little child within her, to help her feel welcome in the world, and to give herself the love she always needed. She has since taken control of her life and healed the victim patterns. Dramatic changes can be made with age regressions.

104

Chapter 12
Treatment of Victim Patterns

> Guilt and helplessness and low self-esteem all work together in a
> vicious cycle to keep the victim a victim, dragging the person further
> and further into the victim triangle like a whirlpool.

Changing Helplessness to Assertiveness

There are several specific parts of the personality of the victim which can
be affected with hypnosis by accessing the subconscious mind. The first is
the pattern of *learned helplessness*.[3] Research has shown that this is one of
the most difficult patterns to break. But with hypnotherapy, it can be done.

Helplessness is taught to children from a very young age by their
rescuing parent. An example is the over-protective parent who tries to do
everything for the child out of the parent's own need to be needed; the
parent who says, "Here, let me do that for you" or "You're too young, let
your brother do it for you." So the child continually gets the message that
somehow because of his/her age, sex ("Girls can't do that" or "Boys
shouldn't do that"), or lack of ability, someone else is needed to do it for
the child. This is literally conditioning someone to be dependent over and
over again.

So the child that grows up being taught to be helpless and dependent is
afraid of many things. These children are afraid to do things on their own,
afraid to take risks and try new things. They learn not to trust their own
instincts, reactions, or abilities. Through hypnotherapy, you can witness
exactly how the child was conditioned to be dependent. Sometimes the
training in helplessness is very overt and obvious and other times it is
much more subtle. Children imitate what they see their parents and older
siblings do. So if a child watches her mother being abused by her father,
she may learn to be a victim just like her mother. That is the unspoken
message, subtle in the sense of being implicit rather than explicit.

Spoken messages may also be ways of teaching the child how to act.
For example, the mother may say, "Now be quiet when Daddy comes
home, we don't want to upset him," or "You know we can't afford that,
stop asking me for things!" These two messages tell the child to become
invisible and don't ask for what you want.

In treating the helplessness, first we go back and observe how it was
taught. We use the subconscious mind as a scanner to sift through years of

experiences and pull out the ones that have led to the helpless feelings. This is an easy task for the subconscious mind to do.

Then the job of re-parenting comes into play. The person develops new images of a new parent who would be more assertive and would encourage assertiveness in the child. These new images can be "programmed" into the mind, and should be recorded on an audiotape for the client to be replayed many times at home.

The helpless patterns also need to be changed on a day-to-day level. This can be done by a method called *hypnobehavioral* therapy, which utilizes behavior modification techniques within the hypnotic trance to increase their effectiveness.[9] It is a method of extinguishing the feelings of fear which prevent the victim from being assertive.

For example, if a woman had been slapped every time she asked for money as a child, she would develop an actual physical response of fear or anxiety around asking for money. This emotional response can be "extinguished" by using hypnobehavioral therapy. This frees the woman to be able to make more assertive responses now. It is that internalized feeling of fear or anxiety which prevents people from responding in assertive ways. When the underlying conditioned response is eliminated, choice is returned and new responses become possible.

Moving from Self-pity to Self-esteem

The feelings of self-pity are so deeply ingrained in the emotional system of the victim person that again hypnosis is the most effective way to really get down to the origin of these feelings. This can be done by going back to the most recent time the person felt sorry for him/herself and then using an emotional bridge to go back to the origin of those feelings.

One way that children learn self-pity is when, as babies, they look at the faces of the adults around them who feel sorry for them. One man named Stan described a scene where he was a baby and all the relatives felt sorry for him because his parents were alcoholics. The parents were always fighting and abusing each other and everyone just knew that Stan was going to have a difficult time. So he learned to feel sorry for himself. Predictably, pity looked like love to him.

Once you can get back to some of these original scenes, the treatment process then involves the "informed child" process. In this technique you inform the child that pity is not love and that you are going to teach the child what real love is all about. You have the person create a new adult who loves the child with respect rather than pity, a parent who appreciates the inner qualities of the child. This is all accomplished in hypnotherapy so that the pictures are changed on the *subconscious* level, in the child ego state in which the original images were created.

On the emotional level, the person may have to express a lot of self-pity and tears, and may have to go down to the depths of feeling sorry for himself before becoming ready to give it up. In fact, the philosopher and author Gurdjieff says that suffering is the last thing people are willing to let go of; they hold on to their suffering tightly. So victims may need to wallow around in their self-pity until they see that it doesn't serve them to do so. When they realize that self-pity is the opposite of self-esteem, they become aware of how non-productive the pity is. When they really start to experience the self-love and how good it feels, it is then much easier to give up the suffering.

In victim families there is a belief in suffering. It is absolutely necessary to get down to the root of these beliefs and change them, to inform the victim that there is no virtue in suffering, and that it will not get anyone to heaven any quicker.

Another ideology which must be changed is the one stating that self-love is selfish and bad. In many victim families there is little, if any, praise for accomplishments. When family members care for themselves or seem to like themselves, they are criticized for being arrogant or selfish.

In actuality, the more love people feel for themselves, the more love they can give to others and the less selfish they are. Being selfish comes from feeling a lack or scarcity and thus being afraid to give for fear of losing what little you have. If you don't feel any love inside of you, it is impossible to give it to others. All love begins with loving yourself inside. This doesn't mean being "stuck" on yourself or being self-centered; it just means having a deep, quiet, accepting love within you.

Turning from Blame to Personal Power

As mentioned before, a common thread in the victim syndrome is blaming everyone and everything outside of yourself for what is happening in your own life. This is a manifestation of the internal feeling of helplessness or powerlessness. The more you see your life as being determined by someone other than you, the more helpless you feel.

During the treatment process, it is very important to go back and begin to see how these patterns of blame were instilled into the child's mind. During an age regression, the person will usually go back to one of several different scenes. A typical one is both parents fighting and somehow blaming the children for their problems. "If we didn't have all these damn kids, we could probably get ahead financially," or "If you hadn't gone and gotten pregnant with that last kid, we'd have enough time to do some of the things we always wanted to."

Another example of learning the blame game is a parent who comes home and is immediately looking to blame someone for something. "Okay, who left the peanut butter jar on the counter?" or "Who is it that is always leaving the refrigerator door open?" With these families the *search is always on* for who to blame for something. The families who play this game of blame for superficial things also play it for much more serious matters.

So the child in this family becomes very defensive, always throwing the hot potato into someone else's lap. "It wasn't my fault" or "I didn't do it" becomes the common denial. "She did it." The habit of always denying responsibility and looking for someone else to blame becomes so ingrained that it is second nature to search for a way to shirk responsibility.

Victims even get into blaming themselves with self-talk statements like, "You know you shouldn't have done that. How could you have been so stupid?" Self-blame is critical and usually elicits shame. It is much different than taking responsibility for your life.

In the treatment process, we must help victims see how they have been giving away their power by blaming others, and to begin to take back that power by accepting full responsibility for their lives. The blame response can be extinguished in the subconscious mind and in this way removed from influence over the conscious mind.

Affirmations are very helpful in reinforcing these new concepts and in re-programming the computer of the mind. A good affirmation here is, "*I, (name), am 100% accountable for what I attract into my life.*" This may be a difficult concept for some people to accept. It cannot be proven to be true or false, but it teaches an individual how to take a position of power in one's life. The affirmation that the victim has been using is, "It's not my fault, poor me. Look what everyone is doing to me."

By changing the victim affirmations to statements of strength, victims will begin to take back their power. Every statement that we make is an affirmation of some type, either positive or negative. You need to become aware of what you say, because that is a reflection of your internal subconscious attitudes.

Changing Guilt to Forgiveness

Guilt is an emotion which is used a great deal in the victim family. Guilt trips are used by the rescuer to try to control and manipulate the children and other family members. Guilt is also used by the persecutor to persecute the family members. Victims are terribly vulnerable to guilt because they feel so helpless and have such low self-esteem.

Guilt and helplessness and low self-esteem all work together in a vicious cycle to keep the person a victim. The more guilt you feel, the lower your self-esteem and then you feel even more helpless. This negative vicious cycle just keeps going round and round and dragging the person further and further into the victim triangle like a whirlpool. Therefore, it is an important part of therapy to extinguish the guilt.

Using the feeling bridge, you can begin with the most recent time that you felt guilty and then take that bridge back to the beginning of those feelings. This will be most interesting because for the first time you will be able to observe and feel how you were infused with guilt from a very early age.

The guilt trips may have been plainly obvious and clearly stated or they may have been subtle and unspoken. An obvious one would be the religious type of guilt that is used on children such as, "How could you do something like that? God is going to punish you if you keep doing that."

The more subtle guilt trips come from contemptuous looks that make you feel guilty or deep, long-suffering sighs. They may also just be implied, like the suffering mother who never buys herself anything and then saves up her grocery money each week all year to buy the child a present. The mother may not say anything, but if this is a victim family, the child will get the guilt message.

Some children are made to feel guilty for playing and laughing and having too much fun. Others are made to feel guilty because they are smarter or prettier than the other siblings. Some children are made to feel guilty just because they exist. These are the people who usually contemplate or attempt suicide in their lives. It may be that they were an accidental pregnancy or unwanted for some reason. Such persons will go around apologizing for themselves all the time. They are apologizing for their existence; they feel guilty for just being alive.

In treatment these people first observe how they were made to feel guilty. On the emotional level it is also important for them to experience the guilt and to realize that it no longer serves them to hold onto it. You can use the extinguishing process to eliminate the guilt response.

It takes extensive work to eliminate deep-seated guilt feelings. Through the extinguishing process they will realize that they can control the guilt feelings. They will also feel much lighter without the burden of guilt. Eliminating guilt is essential in changing the victim pattern. Once the guilt is eliminated, victims can begin to forgive themselves for whatever they were feeling guilty about.

Forgiveness comes a lot easier when the guilt is gone; forgiveness for existing, or for not being perfect, or for being the wrong sex, or for whatever it was that they felt they did wrong.

Along with forgiving yourself, you need to also forgive the others in your life whom you perceive as having harmed you. This is not something that comes from an intellectual decision, but rather from an emotional place inside, a place that you get to after having gone through all the guilt and blame and anger. You finally get to a place in your heart where you know that these people who were your parents did only what they knew how to do at the time. When this place of forgiveness truly comes into your heart, then all the blame and guilt are automatically released!

Changing Approval from Others to Approval from Within

The victim person has come from a codependent family where the children have been taught to be concerned about what other people think of you. There is a big concern for keeping up appearances and putting on an act for everyone outside of the family (see diagram on page 11). Consequently, a false self begins to develop, along with a schism between the true inner self and the false outer self.

The problem with this dichotomy is that the person soon forgets who the real self is. This comes from all the early "don't" messages. Don't be, don't feel, and don't talk about it. Children learn very early to shut down selected parts of themselves and to pretend. So the pretense is the false self and soon becomes the only part of us we are familiar with. The real self has been numbed out and repressed, and this is when many people turn to addictions to keep the inner self numb and under control.

In treatment it becomes vital to stop looking to others for approval, to accept the idea that it really doesn't matter what others think of you, as long as you feel good about your actions. You can't please all of the people all of the time, and it is healthy to stop trying. A good affirmation for this is, "What others think of me is none of my business."

Children have grown up being asked over and over, "What would the neighbors think?" It was so important to get approval from the neighbors and the relatives and the teachers. So the child within us needs to be re-programmed to stop worrying or even caring what others think. This must be done on the subconscious level, in the child ego state.

On an emotional level the treatment involves going back to the times when you were taught to please everyone else, and then to re-train that child within to know that he or she doesn't have to perform for anyone else and that it really doesn't matter what the neighbors think. He or she doesn't have to pretend to be a false self. You then begin encouraging the child within to express the real feelings, the true self.

The Personal Transformation Process

For so many of you who have grown up in dysfunctional families, real feelings have been deeply buried. The real feelings may be completely unknown to you. Through hypnosis and getting down to the subconscious emotional level, you can truly know what you feel. Once this happens it is much easier to accept yourself and your feelings, and to stop caring what others think. The real self emerges and the false phony self dissolves. This is the process of personal transformation.

The personal transformation process is one of the most exciting experiences that you will ever have. It is as though you have been a caterpillar for many years knowing there was a butterfly inside somewhere, but not knowing how to reach that beautiful part of yourself. You have drawn yourself into a cocoon as protection from the pain and hurt. The problem is that the cocoon is a very lonely place, cramped and limiting. As you begin your therapy, you begin the process of emerging from that cocoon as the beautiful butterfly, the real self.

This transformation process may continue for years or it may continue for the rest of your life. It is exciting because it involves self-discovery and becoming more alive, activating passion for life and compassion for oneself and for others. For many people it develops into a spiritual transformation. You can't control it or force yourself to go any faster than you can go. So just sit back and enjoy the journey.

Use the questionnaire on the following page to become more clear about the healthy love and any codependency in your significant relationships.

111

DEFINING HEALTHY LOVE & CODEPENDENCY

Check the first box if this describes how you feel toward your significant relationships.
Check the second box if this describes how your significant relationships feel about you.

CODEPENDENCY (victim/rescuer)

❏ ❏ 1. Pity - I feel sorry for you - and that feels like love to me

❏ ❏ 2. I love you the most when you are the weakest

❏ ❏ 3. What attracted me to you is your helplessness/ pain/ weakness/ neediness

❏ ❏ 4. I feel responsible for fixing you and that feels like love to me

HEALTHY LOVE

❏ ❏ 1. I greatly respect and admire you

❏ ❏ 2. My self-esteem has improved as a result of being in a relationship with you

❏ ❏ 3. I feel equal to you in our relationship (not one up/one down. Not parent/child)

❏ ❏ 4. I am loved for who I am, not for what I give or produce

Chapter 13
Changing the Pattern of Rescuing

The feeling of *guilt* attracts *punishment.* Because guilt is a major weapon in the victim triangle, illness often becomes the self-inflicted punishment that follows.

If the dominant part of your personality seems to fall into the category of rescuer, then there are certain response patterns that need to be changed. You may wonder, what is wrong with being a rescuer? Many people tell me that they like to help people and they don't want to feel that anything is wrong with it.

It is true that helping people is a wonderful trait. But the rescuer does it to the detriment of the other person, as well as to himself. You must remember that rescuers will always attract victims and those victims will end up persecuting the rescuers. Also, the rescuer always ends up *super stressed out* from taking on the responsibility for the problems of others.

Remember, rescuers "help" others because they feel so powerless themselves. It is an attempt to feel "one-up" on those a little less together than they are. It is an attempt to eliminate the underlying victim feeling and to appear stronger than others.

Releasing Responsibility for Others

In the treatment of the rescuer, it is important to take the person back to where all this started. The rescuer is often the first or an only child. They have usually been made to feel responsible for younger siblings, often at a very early age. Another common situation is a dysfunctional family where the child sees the parent(s) as helpless victim(s) and somehow tries to take responsibility for them, lift their burden, or "fix" them. The child may see the mother getting abused by the father, or may see one of the parents as drug- or alcohol-addicted.

Obviously the child can't fix the parent, and therefore comes to feel quite helpless. This exaggerated sense of responsibility is called *parentification*, defined as an on-going family pattern in which a child is excessively and inappropriately assigned roles and responsibilities normally reserved for adults, i.e., taking care of adults and/or siblings.[10] These persons go through their lives attracting other people to fix in an attempt to remedy their self-blame for not fixing their parents.

113

They must go back to the original situation where they felt responsible for fixing things, which is done in the hypnotherapy session. When they go through several of these early situations in age regressions, they begin to see the pattern and how it developed in their lives. They must be able to see how detrimental this pattern has been in their lives. Often they have attracted one victim after another to fix, and these relationships usually end in resentment or disaster.

Then they must return to the original child scene where the rescuing pattern first began. The child must be informed at this point that he is not responsible for the grown-ups, and that burden must be lifted. It is usually a big relief when the person feels freed from this original unrealistic and impossible responsibility.

They also need to go back to each victim situation that they have attracted in their lifetime, and release themselves from responsibility. This is a long process and will take several sessions.

Knowing that Your Needs are Important

The rescuer has grown up in a dysfunctional family where there has been a special needs person, usually the victim, who received most of the attention. So if you are a rescuer, you learned that your needs would come second or third or probably not be met at all. You became used to just discounting what you needed in order to take care of someone else. To the rescuer it feels normal to get fulfillment indirectly, through taking care of someone else. Your fulfillment has been vicarious rather than direct.

The problem with this is that the rescuer begins to feel unfulfilled and somewhat resentful. These feelings build up over years and years of unmet needs and the rescuer may express these resentments by switching over to the persecutor role. This may take the form of anger, but more often it is expressed through guilt trips and manipulation.

The guilt trips may be very destructive, such as getting sick or injured so that someone will take care of you. Since the rescuer has a difficult time accepting love, love will often be confused with pity. Getting sick means being taken care of, and can attract sympathy which looks like caring. The rescuer often plays the martyr for this purpose.

The treatment for this rescuer part of the personality begins with being direct. You must learn to know what your needs are and then directly ask for those needs to be met. This is very difficult for rescuers because they have spent years discounting their needs. In hypnotherapy, you will easily be able to get in touch with your needs that have been suppressed.

The basic needs which usually come out are the needs to be loved and nurtured. A typical rescuer named Phyllis went back in hypnotherapy to her birth experience. At that time, her mother's mother was recovering from breast cancer. The mother felt that she could not care for both, so she took care of her mother and sent the baby away to be cared for by another relative. When Phyllis finally was returned home at age two, she then was trained to care for her grandmother with cancer. She learned to receive praise for taking care of others. She learned that the praise she received had to be earned through serving someone else.

Phyllis grew up feeling that her own needs to be loved and taken care of were not important. She learned that the only way she could get something that looked like love, and to avoid rejection and exile, was to take care of someone. She also learned that love was conditional and had to be earned rather than just freely given, unconditionally. Not surprisingly, she had a pattern of attracting men into her life who could not meet her emotional needs.

In the hypnotherapy, it is vitally important to see what the pattern is and how rescuers have been trained to feel that their needs will not be met. They must be informed that they certainly do deserve to have their needs met and that the situation is now different than it was when they were young. This may take some convincing and several sessions of re-informing the child.

Taking Responsibility to Have Your Needs Met

The next phase of the therapy involves learning what the needs are and asking directly to have those needs met. This takes awareness as well as assertiveness. Both of these become a part of the therapy process and are most effectively accomplished in an intensive group process (discussed later).

Eliminating Guilt Trips

Guilt trips must be eliminated in the next phase of treatment. The rescuer can go back to how guilt trips were used in the family to control behavior. This response can be extinguished through hypnobehavioral therapy. The new response to be learned and programmed is *clear and direct communication*.

Guilt is pervasive throughout each phase of the victim triangle. The rescuer is usually filled with guilt. Because rescuers have been systematically taught to discount their needs, they feel guilty for having them. They also feel guilty if they are not always busily engaged in meeting everyone else's needs.

The guilt can easily be traced back to guilt trips laid on the person from early childhood, usually used to control and manipulate the child in many different areas. The child who is placed into the role of rescuer has been made to feel guilty simply for thinking of himself. This is judged as selfishness. The child is also made to feel guilty about expressing any feelings. So any real expression of how the child feels is stifled.

An example is a young man named Fred who came into my office for marital problems. In the hypnotherapy, Fred went back to being five years old and wanting to play with his friends. Daily his mother dragged him with her shopping, telling him that she was lonesome and needed his company. Here she is using guilt to have the little boy discount his needs in order to rescue his mother. She also lied and told him it would only take a few minutes, when in fact it lasted most of the afternoon. When the child finally couldn't take being dragged from clothes store to clothes store, he became angry and threw a tantrum on the floor. Here is where the real guilt in the form of shame came about. The mother screamed, "How could you embarrass me in front of my friends like this?" Little Fred was shamed for expressing his feelings in the only way available to him.

In hypnosis, the patterns of guilt and shame can easily be located. Treatment must extinguish the guilt and let the rescuer part of the personality know that it is okay to have needs, to have those needs met and to express your feelings. The rescuer usually feels a great release when this burden of guilt is lifted, allowing for acceptance of her own needs as legitimate.

Releasing the Anger

The next step in the treatment of the rescuer is to release the anger underneath the guilt. Because the child was not allowed to express feelings, especially anger, the rescuer has a huge reservoir of pent-up anger. Many times the person seems "sweet as pie" on the outside. They are totally unaware of their anger because they have spent their whole lives being a good little girl or boy. Remember, rescuers are "people pleasers." But deeply buried underneath that sweet exterior is a lot of rage.

In the hypnotherapy, when the guilt trips become obvious, the anger begins to surface. This is the time to have the person express his feelings in a healthy way. I have them yell into a pillow, hit down on the floor with

116

a rubber hose, or make a fist and punch into a vinyl or leather pillow. This can all be done while still in the trance. In fact, for many people it may even deepen the trance to finally acknowledge and express true feelings.

The Healthy Release of Anger

Learning to release anger in a healthy way is one very important step towards recovery. Expressing it in the hypnotherapy diminishes inhibitions about it. The expression usually brings a big release from the internal pressure, and feels so liberating to the person that some key changes begin to manifest. If, however, releasing the anger instead rekindles the old guilt, then that guilt must be extinguished again.

There are several reasons why the healthy release of anger is so important. Most people in victim families saw either one extreme or the other. Either anger was totally repressed and the phony "happy family" face was plastered on everyone, especially to the outside world, or the anger was taken out on someone in the family in the form of emotional or physical abuse. There was no healthy medium from one extreme of repression to the other of abuse.

Another reason why healthy expression of anger is so important is that many rescuers turn this anger inward and become seriously depressed. It is often a clue that anger is present when the person is depressed and may be doing self-destructive behaviors, including contemplating or attempting suicide. It takes a lot of energy to hold this anger in so that the rescuer often feels very low energy, exhausted and overwhelmed. When the anger is released in a healthy way, the energy returns and the depression disappears.

The person needs to release anger on a regular basis, since pent-up anger does not dissipate in one experience of expressing it. The individual is learning and practicing tools to release anger on an as-needed basis. The therapist provides permission to do what was never before allowed: healthy expression and release of anger.

If anger is not expressed overtly, many people express it covertly, in a passive-aggressive way. There are a million ways that people covertly express anger. To express anger covertly, someone may "accidentally" bang up your car or make you wait for a half hour or procrastinate on a job they promised. I'd much rather hear the direct expression of the anger than to feel the covert "jabs."

One type of covert expression of anger is turning it into illness. You've heard the expression "his anger was eating away at him." People

117

who repress anger can actually turn it into physical illnesses, like cancer, which is a physical manifestation of "the eating away." Some people subconsciously turn unexpressed anger into illness in order to suffer, so they can become a martyr. This way they can use guilt to control and punish other people (moving into the persecutor role). Anger can also manifest as illness when there is a lot of personal guilt and the person is punishing himself. The feeling of *guilt* attracts *punishment.* Because guilt is a major weapon in the victim triangle, illness often becomes the self-inflicted punishment that follows. This is a very unhealthy pattern and usually leads to unnecessary illness and suffering, and may end in premature death.

Anger and Addictions

The rescuer is often involved in addictions as a means of suppressing emotions, especially anger. Because rescuers are so involved in denying their own needs and taking care of everyone else, a great deal of resentment builds up. In order to continue to play the role of "having it all together," they must numb themselves to the feelings that get in the way. So food, sugar, drugs, alcohol and tobacco are used to numb the anger and keep the game going.

In treatment, when the rescuer begins to release this anger, the addictions can be released. I have treated so many clients with weight problems who saw incredible results with weight loss once they began to express their anger.

I have noticed that the stronger the addiction, the more anger there is to release. For example, people who are very much overweight have often been abused by a persecutor. Also, many people with strong cocaine addictions have a lot of anger they are holding in.

I can't emphasize enough how important this work is for people who have weight problems. In my weight release program, I have seen the victim triangle at work over and over again. No matter how many weight release programs you attend, if you don't deal with these issues, the weight will never stay off permanently.

I have found that it is crucial for therapists to not only feel comfortable with expressing their own anger, but to be releasing it on a regular basis themselves. It's been my experience that hypnosis and breathwork are both excellent tools for this release work (see the discussion on breathwork in chapter 15).

Releasing Responsibility for Others, Becoming Responsible for Oneself

At this point, the rescuers are releasing guilt, expressing anger, and beginning to know what their own needs are. When this happens, they must now hold other people able to handle their own lives. In other words, to let go! This is often very difficult for the rescuer because they have usually gotten all of their self-worth from taking care of others. Often, in fact, the rescuer developed the belief that no one else can do it; *if it is to be done, I must do it.*

The problem is that rescuers do more than take care of others; they "take on" the problems of others. So at first, when the rescuer begins to hold others able to run their own lives, he or she may feel useless and empty. They have always needed others to be dependent on them. This is the codependency. So to let go of being needed is very scary. The idea, however, is to let go of taking care of others and to begin taking care of oneself.

This is a whole new learning process for the rescuer, and the therapy must continue while the new person begins to emerge. People frequently ask, "Does this mean that I can't care about other people?" The answer is, of course you can care about people. Caring is a wonderful trait. The idea is to be able to support others in solving *their own* problems, rather than attempting to do it for them.

This is very important in all relationships such as parent/ child, husband/ wife, and client/ therapist. Both people in the relationship must define their own boundaries and take responsibility for what is theirs.

Giving Others Back Their Power, Claiming Your Power

This is really the crux of the whole issue. If you look at the illustration of the victim triangle, the center of the triangle is a *lack of power*. So when the blame and guilt are extinguished and the anger is released in a healthy way, the person can begin to take back the personal power in his/her life.

Real transformation comes as a person learns to be powerful. When you learn that being powerful does not mean hurting others, you begin to see that you don't gain your power at the expense of others; it does not take anything away from anyone else. In fact, the more powerful you become, the easier it is for you to affirm success in others. You will then begin to attract other powerful people into your life.

The victim consciousness is really the consciousness of failure. You may not find yourself failing in all areas of your life, but there is no need to fail at all. For example, some people are very successful at work, but have one failed relationship after another. Some people are successful at work and relationships, but can't seem to break an addiction to a substance. The person who has broken the vicious cycle of the victim triangle, however, is successful in all areas of life.

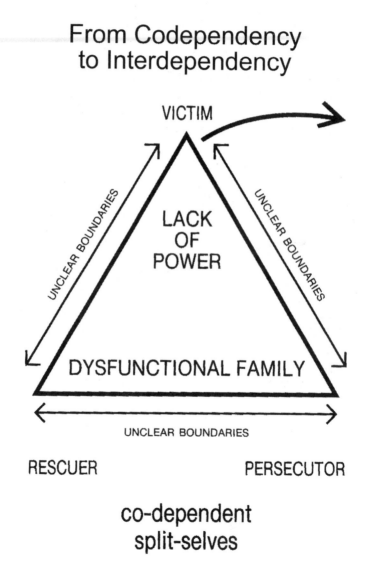

From Codependency to Interdependency

VICTIM

LACK OF POWER

UNCLEAR BOUNDARIES

UNCLEAR BOUNDARIES

DYSFUNCTIONAL FAMILY

UNCLEAR BOUNDARIES

RESCUER   PERSECUTOR

co-dependent
split-selves

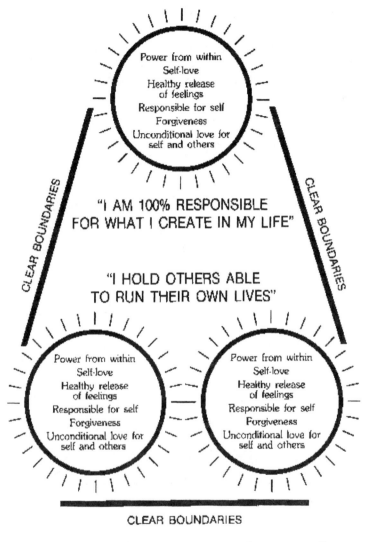

Power from within
Self-love
Healthy release
of feelings
Responsible for self
Forgiveness
Unconditional love for
self and others

CLEAR BOUNDARIES

CLEAR BOUNDARIES

"I AM 100% RESPONSIBLE
FOR WHAT I CREATE IN MY LIFE"

"I HOLD OTHERS ABLE
TO RUN THEIR OWN LIVES"

Power from within
Self-love
Healthy release
of feelings
Responsible for self
Forgiveness
Unconditional love for
self and others

Power from within
Self-love
Healthy release
of feelings
Responsible for self
Forgiveness
Unconditional love for
self and others

CLEAR BOUNDARIES

Healthy Family: Interdependency

Changing the Pattern of Rescuing

Chapter 14
Healing the Persecutor Personality

In victim families shame is used when the parents bring out the heavy
artillery in the battle for control and power.

All the treatment aspects that we have discussed so far about the victim
also apply to the persecutor. Remember, as reflected on the diagram, the
persecutor feels like a victim underneath his or her "tough" exterior. When
I say tough, this can be taken in one of two ways. The person can appear
to be "tough" as in macho or they can appear to be tough as in strong and
having it all together. The word "appear" is important here, for this is all
just an act. Underneath the tough exterior, the persecutor feels as helpless
as any victim who is crumbling right before your eyes.

Many times men take the role of persecutors because this is what they
have been taught through cultural beliefs like "big boys don't cry," and
"stand up and fight like a man." Young boys learn the role of persecution
from a very young age. Watch what happens on a children's playground,
where the boys constantly persecute the girls or the weaker boys through
teasing; these kids then take the role of the victim, crying and telling the
teachers (rescuers).

This does not mean that women do not get into the roles of
persecutors, but they usually do it in a different way. Men often persecute
directly by physical, verbal or sexual abuse; or they persecute indirectly by
emotional or financial withdrawal, or by going out and getting drunk.
Women may use abuse or addictions to persecute, but are often more adept
at persecuting with guilt. Both men and women use sex as their sword.
Money is another weapon used to control and hurt each other.

This is not the place to get into the battle of the sexes, but I want to
make it clear that there are many different ways to persecute each other.
Couples involved in going back and forth between victim and persecutor
can drive themselves and everyone around them crazy! It is a never-
ending battle and everyone and anything may be used as pawns in this
sinister game.

The treatment goes much faster if both people are involved directly in
it. Because the source of the problem is feeling powerless, these battles are
coming from two people who are using each other to try to feel powerful.
If one can get control of the other person in some area, then somehow there

is more satisfaction in that person's own life. This, of course, is untrue and merely an illusion, but it is nevertheless the *modus operandi* of persecutors.

Persecutors must first and foremost get down to the core of their anger and learn to express it in the therapy office in a healthy way. Persecutors have learned to express their anger in unhealthy ways by taking it out on others. This is an unacceptable release of anger and must be re-directed to the floor or a pillow or a punching bag.

If persecutors are the type who abuse through withdrawal, or what we call *passive aggression*, then they must learn to express the anger overtly in the therapy office first. This may be very difficult for persecutors, because they are so fearful of their anger. Unlike rescuers, who are totally unaware of their anger, persecutors know it's there and fear its destructive power.

The persecutor is afraid of this anger because at one time or another he has used it to hurt someone or has felt the desire to hurt someone with it. From that time on, the persecutor may have held it in and may be like a volcano about to explode! This becomes a self-fulfilling prophesy because the more the person holds the anger in, the more likely he is to explode. And then the explosiveness justifies his fear of his anger.

With regular, healthy expressions of the inner rage, the person actually becomes less dangerous because the pressure valve is released. Persecutors are no longer afraid of the anger and actually feel much more in control of their lives.

In therapy, people begin to own their feelings and discover where the feelings originated. Most of the rage we have goes back to childhood, and we have just attracted a series of people to re-create the scenes with. In hypnotherapy, you can go back to the source of the anger and release it in healthy ways.

Releasing Blame

Another important part of treatment is to let go of the blame. In every phase of the victim triangle, blame continues to lead to a feeling of more helplessness. If the persecutor continues to feel that someone is "doing it to him," then he continues to feel out of control.

If on the highest level of consciousness, the person can realize that we all create our own reality, then it is much easier to release the blame. In order to release the victim consciousness, you must take the position of the winner which is, *"I am 100% accountable for what I attract into my life."*

124

When you realize this truth, then and only then do you take back personal power in your life. Use this affirmation twenty-five times a day until you completely internalize it.

Every person in our life has been put into our life to teach us something. We have attracted everyone in our life, our parents, our friends, our enemies, to learn from them whatever our lessons are. As long as we learn from these situations, no matter how painful they have been, then the victim triangle will be released from our consciousness.

The healing of persecutors directly depends on their ability to stop blaming others and to take back the power in their lives. They will then realize that being powerful does not mean having power over someone else. A good affirmation for this position is, *"My power comes from within."*

Extinguishing Addictions

The persecutor personality may be very much involved in using addictions not only to numb feelings but to "get back" at the other person. The addictions may be sexual, substance abuse, or spending. As the therapy progresses, these addictions must be extinguished. As long as the persecutor is "using" (indulging the addiction) as a way to punish, they are still trapped in victimization.

The victim triangle (refer to the diagram on page 120) is a true picture of how unclear the boundaries can get within the victim relationship. The people constantly go back and forth between the different roles with lightning speed. The boundaries between each individual person are so foggy that a clear sense of identity is difficult.

Since the victim personality is present underneath each position, all the family members seem to be confused about who they truly are. Also, because so much guilt is used to control, the individual members do not know what they really want. The individuals are so involved in the family games and cover-ups that clear, independent individuality is not present.

In the recovery process, a whole new individual person will begin to emerge. This is personal transformation. You will know who you are separate from your parents or your spouse or your children. Developing clear boundaries is inevitable when you hold others able to run their own lives and when you take full responsibility for yours (see diagram of healthy family relationships on page 121).

Healing Shame

In many aspects of the victim triangle, the issue of shame comes up. It is especially prevalent in the use of guilt to control. I have used the word guilt, but in many families the word shame could be used. John Bradshaw covers this subject thoroughly in his book, *Healing the Shame That Binds You.* Shame exists on a much deeper level than guilt and is far more devastating.

In victim families shame is used when the parents bring out the heavy artillery in the battle for control and power. It is devastating to the children and follows them for the rest of their life. The good news is that shame can be extinguished and released.

Take time with the questionnaire on the following page to become more clear about eliminating persecuting patterns from your life.

BREAKING FREE FROM THE VICTIM PATTERN:
Eliminating Persecuting Patterns

1. What feelings/emotions do you push down?

2. What feelings/emotions do you "dump" on others (i.e., unhealthy expression)?

3. What feelings/emotions do you use addictions to numb?

4. Are you willing to find new *healthy* ways to express these feelings?

Healing the Persecutor Personality

Chapter 15
Healing the Victim Personality

Healing the victim personality means the adult provides safety for the inner child, lost for so long, to reconnect, to trust, to express true feelings, and to return to spontaneous innocence.

Once the victim patterns are released, the doors open for you to truly become who you are. You will know on a very deep level what you feel, what you want, and exactly how to manifest it in your life. You will no longer be seeking approval from outside yourself. You will have the quiet confidence to experience the profound, authentic approval from within. You will be reunited with the spontaneous child within you as well as with the wise adult who makes clear decisions and wise choices. There will also be a loving nurturing parent inside that provides inner confidence.

The child within all of us is the spontaneous, fun-loving part who loves to play and laugh. I'm not talking about the nervous laugh that some use to cover up their fears. I'm talking about the free, spontaneous laughter of the child within. Sometime during childhood, many people abandoned or split from the child part as a protection against feeling pain. So many young children were "parentified" by having to do excessive chores, taking responsibility way beyond their years for other siblings and even for the adults who may have been drinking or were in some other way incapacitated and dysfunctional.

Ego states: The Nurturing Parent, the Wise Adult, the Spontaneous Child

The healing that we are speaking about involves recognizing that there are actually three separate and distinct ego states or *parts* of ourselves. They live within us and often times *take over* when we don't realize it. An example that you may recognize in yourself has to do with addictive behavior, including addictive relationships. Perhaps your adult part has gotten very clear that it is not healthy for you to be in a certain relationship. You have clearly seen that for years the relationship either doesn't meet your needs or, worse, is physically or emotionally abusive. Perhaps you have worked on this decision to separate for a long time and perhaps even had some professional help to get really clear. The *adult* is very clear that it is time to go. And yet, perhaps you suddenly find yourself on the phone calling up your spouse or partner, apologizing and asking him/her to give the relationship one more try. You hang up the phone and stand there perplexed, wondering where that came from. The *adult* has vanished and the needy, scared little *child* may have taken over. This all happens on an unconscious level, unless you have done the work we are describing in this book. Healing the victim triangle is all about making these ego states conscious and within our reach so that we do, now, have clear choices.

The Adaptive Child vs. the Spontaneous Child

The healing of the victim triangle means the internal reuniting with the child that has been lost for so long. As you reconnect with your true feelings, the spontaneous child feels safer to return. The child ego state can be better understood by watching a real child as well as doing the powerful regressive work that we speak about. A small child can remind us of the natural spontaneous ego part that we want to reclaim in ourselves. This is the part that has often been stifled by well-meaning but uneducated or overly stressed parents. When the natural child is laughing, having fun and being silly, adults will often tell him or her to be quiet and stop making so much noise. In some families and certainly in some schools, corporal punishment is even used to punish the child for having too much fun! For other children who are very sensitive, just a scowling look from an important parent or teacher is enough to send them into fear and shame. As a child you may have gotten these messages so often that you soon learned to stifle that spontaneous part of yourself. You may have been systematically trained *not* to be happy and fun-loving!

The Adaptive Child: Our Shadow Parts

This conditioning process leads to the emergence of what we call the *shadow parts* of the child, or the *adaptive child.* They are called shadow parts because we don't often see them or even know that they exist. They may be just outside our field of vision, in our blind spot. Yet these shadows are often seen and experienced directly by those closest to us. It is here, in the adaptive child ego state, that the victim triangle is formed. These are adaptive ways of behaving, since who we naturally were as children did not seem to please the dysfunctional adults. On a deep subconscious level we had to sell our souls and adapt in order to survive.

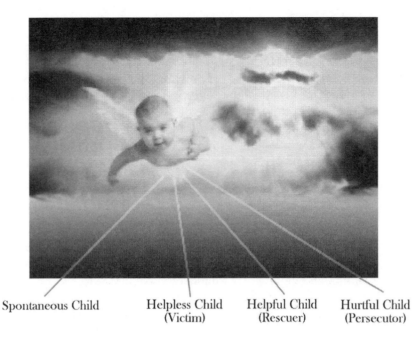

Spontaneous Child   Helpless Child   Helpful Child   Hurtful Child
                         (Victim)   (Rescuer)   (Persecutor)

The Rescuer (Helpful Child)

The helpful child is the child part that learned to be very good in order to avoid the punishment of criticism, blame and rejection, and to attempt to please the adults at all cost. The cost is often very great, indeed, since it involves losing the spontaneous child in order to try to appease the adults. As the individual grows up, the adaptive helpful child puts on a sweet smile to the outside world, becomes the rescuer and pleases the parents and teachers. It is often a surprise when this sweet child, who never got into trouble, at some point suddenly does.

The Persecutor (Hurtful Child)

Inside the very good child, because of paying the price of loss of Self, the rebellious, *hurtful child* often begins to develop. There is an underlying anger which begins to seethe inside, but is usually repressed by the part that is the helpful child. This is the other side of the adaptive child and is the part that always defeats you. This is the persecutor personality we refer to. Perhaps you are in touch with self-sabotage and can't figure out why you keep defeating yourself. Herein lies the answer.

131

The Victim (Helpless Child)

The free, fun-loving, happy child has had to adapt to many injunctions which usually include, "Don't be you," "Don't make noise," "Don't bother anyone," and "Don't tell the family secrets." These injunctions or commands leave the child feeling helpless. When the hurtful child is punished (and they usually are), or when the helpful child is ignored (which they often are in deference to more problematic children), the child feels confused, resentful, and helpless. The helpless child provides the genesis of victim consciousness.

The Wise Adult vs. the Little Professor

Most people think that they have a very strong adult part of themselves that governs their behavior. This may be true for some people. However, if you grew up in a family where you had to take on the role of an adult at a very early age, you may instead have internalized what we call the *little professor*. This is a child trying *to act* like what he or she perceives an adult to be. The little professor often comes across as a know-it-all, bossy and even like a bully. Also because of emotional, physical (including neglect) or sexual abuse there is an absence of a well-functioning adult ego state. When any of these abuses happen, especially in alcoholic families, the children's emotional growth is stunted and they do not develop the mature adult ego state necessary for healthy functioning. In a couple who are fighting, you can actually see their two hurtful and helpless inner children interacting, with no healthy adult present.

The Nurturing Parent vs. the Critical Parent

The nurturing parent is the part of our ego that praises us and that provides the internal sense of knowing that we are loved unconditionally. Since most people have not had many experiences of unconditional love, this is often a difficult concept for them to experience. Most people have internalized, instead, the critical parent who constantly compares your talents with those of others, lets you know all the mistakes you have made today, and lets you know that you don't have the skills to make things any better! This is what so many people heard growing up, day in and day out. Studies show that our subconscious minds are like video recorders; they dutifully record every bit of information, especially if given by a well-loved and perhaps well-meaning parent, nun or teacher. They are also like

132

computers and store all the information in files which is easily retrieved by the critical parent ego state. Sit quietly for a few moments and listen to the negative voices in your head. They probably come from this internalized critical parent.

Ego State Therapy and Healing the Victim, Rescuer and Persecutor

Individual sessions of Heart-Centered Hypnotherapy and the Personal Transformation groups are the methods we have found most effective to accomplish this ego state therapy. There is nothing more healing than to experience several of your shadow parts in clear view and openly interacting with you in a psychodrama. Now you get the opportunity to face them and recognize them for the small children that they actually are. As others role-play the dysfunctional situations that you, as a child, lived through, you can see how the shadow parts were formed. You retrieve the conclusions and decisions that you made as a small child which gave so much power to these adaptive ego states. Suddenly, it is clearly understandable where their (your) needs come from and how these needs can be addressed in healthy ways. You have the opportunity to dialogue with these parts of yourself and resolve issues that were formerly repressed or hidden and are now in your full conscious awareness.

In resolving the ego state issues, we always want to move towards making new, more empowering conclusions and decisions for ourselves. Just as we have mentioned the computer of the subconscious mind before, these early childhood decisions are the programs that are stored in the computer of our minds. A child, after many experiences of being abandoned, may conclude, "No one is ever going to be here for me. It's safer to be alone." Based on that conclusion, the child may decide, "I won't even try." A major aspect of the healing of the ego states is to change the old conclusions and decisions. Sandy's decision as a child to "be good" and "not be noticed," mentioned in chapter 7, formed the basis for her lack of assertiveness as an adult. Changing that decision in therapy changed the early computer programming stored in the subconscious mind.

As the healing work progresses and the issues are resolved, these old decisions are changed. Then there is no longer any need for the adaptive ego states to exist. You reclaim your personal power, replacing the victim child's helplessness with the boldness to speak your truth and express your true feelings. This is not the power of the hurtful child, used to over-power others, but the power of the wise adult, used to realize your full potential.

The child now knows that the adult is there to help handle the feelings. I have many clients re-create a loving nurturing parent to give the inner child what is needed. I have the client become that child. It is profoundly healing when the parent within loves and nurtures the child within.

Expression vs. Repression of Feelings

Learning how to deal with feelings is a very important part of the healing process. In most families around the world, the child is not given the tools she/he needs to express feelings in a healthy way. Over the past thirty years of doing therapeutic work with thousands of people, I have found that for therapy to be most effective, it must actually teach you to identify and express your feelings. Over the twenty years that I have been teaching Heart-Centered Hypnotherapy to other professionals, I have seen that most therapists, themselves, have never learned to express their own emotions in healthy ways. Many of the thousands of therapists I have trained are very grateful to finally have a safe and nurturing place to learn to express their feelings. They can then take these skills back to their clients, who can in turn teach them to their children and spouses.

The diagram on page 136 shows how feelings are usually arranged in layers with the anger on top. The anger is often experienced like a big wet blanket that covers all the other ones. Rage is the result of years and years of anger that has been held in. Once people learn to express their anger in a healthy way, the other feelings become much more accessible. As people release their anger, we usually notice grief, pain and sadness emerge. The love, joy and exuberance are on the bottom of the diagram because those are so often buried underneath the heaviness of the repressed anger. When you release the anger, pain and sadness, you will experience much more love, joy and spiritual connection in your life.

Repression of Emotions

Repression of emotions is one of the major causes of addictions, abuse, depression, and disease in our culture. In many families, emotions are either repressed or expressed in abusive ways. When children indicate a feeling of anger, the parent may punish them or shame them into repressing it. "Go to your room until you can act like a lady," is a common response. This shames the child and makes him/her feel rejected. A healthier response would be to help the child identify the feeling and to

134

release it. "I see you're feeling angry, let's go and punch your punching bag."

Another common response of parents that leads to repression and confusion is denial of the feelings. Whatever the child says they may be feeling, such as angry, sad, or scared, the response of the parent is, "Oh no, you're not feeling that," or "Be a big boy now and stop that!" The child then learns to mistrust their own perceptions and repress what they feel. Children look around at the older people in their lives and their *mental video camera* records what they see for use later on. So they may see their mother using food or tranquilizers to numb her feelings, their father drinking alcohol, an older brother smoking pot or a sister smoking cigarettes. When this child begins to feel his or her own stress, they use one of these coping strategies to numb their own emotions. This is how addictions begin in our lives.

In the diagram, you can see that repression of feelings will lead to many serious complications. Millions of Americans take anti-depressant drugs because our whole society has been taught to repress feelings with drugs. The popular drug Prozac was originally supposed to be prescribed for a course of six months, to be used only in conjunction with psychotherapy. Now it is given out like candy for indefinite periods of time and the therapy recommendation has been long forgotten. When children see this medical model as a role model, then it is obvious why drug addictions are rampant among our youth. Many people are taught to repress their feelings by being shamed for having feelings. The expression "Shame on you" is very common when a child expresses anger. So we are consistently made to feel that our angry feelings (for girls) and our sad or scared feelings (for boys) are shameful. It is extremely unhealthy the way males in our culture have been systematically shamed for their soft tender feelings. This has led to the majority of men in our culture having a very difficult time crying and expressing their grief. I have worked with many men who were easily able to cry during the hypnotherapy and thanked me profusely. Many have said they've never been able to cry as adults. One man told me he couldn't even cry at his own mother's funeral. This has also led to many stress-related symptoms, such as heart attacks and strokes. In Louise Hay's book *You Can Heal Your Life*, she states that heart attacks are often related to unexpressed grief!

When people repress their emotions, there is a tendency to use passive aggression as a way of expressing them. This results in a person who may express his/her anger indirectly, which is called passive aggression. These can be people who smile to your face and then stab you in the back. A common expression in our culture which reflects this concept is, "I don't get mad, I get even!" I would much rather experience healthy direct expression of anger than a continual indirect attack.

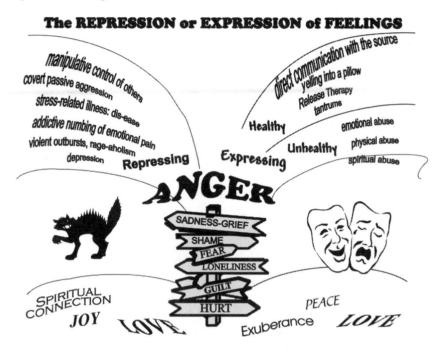

The REPRESSION or EXPRESSION of FEELINGS

Repression of Emotions and Disease

The whole concept of disease or illness is often related to emotions which have been repressed. When a person holds in anger, that angry energy has to go somewhere. Some people hold it in their jaw, others in their chest and some in their stomach. Angry energy can actually be held anywhere and everywhere in the body. This energy, if not released, then does violence to the body itself, in the form of disease. So the person that holds in their feelings and does not say what needs to be said, may experience tension in the jaw which can result in TMJ or grinding of the teeth. The person with ulcers or stomach or colon cancer perhaps has held unexpressed anger in that area of the body for many years. The person with breast cancer may have rescued and taken care of everyone else but herself for many years and held the resentment inside of her body. The breast, after all, is the part of the body that represents a woman's nurturing of others. The word *dis-ease* means an uneasiness somewhere in the body.

If you have a disease, ask yourself, "What is the uneasiness in my life?" People often transfer their emotional pain into physical pain because it may be easier to say, "My stomach hurts" than to say "I hurt."

Unhealthy Expression of Emotions

Many people find it difficult at first when we teach them to express their feelings in healthy ways. In fact, they often react with embarrassment and say, "Oh, I can't do that. I don't want to be violent." The most common reason for this reaction is that most people have been shamed for any outward expression of emotions. However, there is also a whole group of folks who grew up in families where one or more of their parents were rage-aholics. Perhaps you grew up in a family where someone yelled or threw things on a regular basis. In some families children are whipped with belts, paddles or switches. There is a fine line between discipline and abuse, and too often parents cross that line with their children when they themselves lose their temper. Also, most of our parents were never taught good parenting skills and had no role modeling for good discipline. In many families rage is dumped on other people, which is seen as normal. This happens most often when alcohol is involved and then all hell breaks loose. When we ask adults raised in alcoholic or abusive families to express their emotions, they immediately bring that rage to mind. They associate what we are asking them to do with the rage-aholic abuse that happened in their families. That is why they say, "I don't want to be violent." If their parents had done Heart-Centered Hypnotherapy, and had been taught to express feelings in healthy ways, they would not have shamed their children or dumped their angry feelings on them.

Healthy Expression of Feelings

The first step in healthy expression of feelings is to learn to label what we feel. Most people don't even have words for the intense emotional reactions that go on in their bodies. We always ask people to learn the core emotions: anger, fear, hurt, sadness, loneliness and shame. That way they begin to have a vocabulary for what is going on inside them. Then as they speak about a situation, or some feeling, we always ask them to locate where and how they experience the feelings as sensations in the body. This helps to really be able to know when the feelings are strong, when they are reduced and when they are released. Feelings are also the very powerful bridges that take you back to childhood memories and

137

experiences. Sometimes we call them *body memories.* Even if your conscious mind has dissociated from a memory because it was too painful to remember, your body remembers it.

What is the difference between healthy expression of feelings and abuse or violence? This is a very important question. Healthy expression of feelings gets the angry, hurt or scared energy out of your body without hurting property, yourself or any other person. It can be an intense release using the voice by yelling into a pillow, and perhaps using an energy release hose on a punching bag. The angry energy is always focused on the punching bag, and is in that way very safe for all involved. In all the years that I have done this work, I have always had great results from introducing the energy release hose to people from all walks of life and from all over the world. Once people got over their embarrassment or fear, they usually love the feeling of power, release and freedom they feel when they get the stuck energy moving in their bodies. I have witnessed amazing emotional and physical healings too numerous to mention here, once people let out what has become body armor for most of their lives.

Another great way to release pent up stress and frustration is to have a tantrum on your bed. Most children do this naturally when they feel frustrated. The problem is that we have shamed children for doing this and so they turn it around and shame us by having a tantrum in public at the grocery store or the doctor's office. Instead, a healthier approach is to teach them the value of the tantrum and help them identify their feelings. The first time they have a tantrum, get right down on the floor with them and look them in the eye and say, "It looks like you are feeling very mad right now. So let's pound on this pillow (or whatever is available and appropriate) and get that anger out of your body. Mommy will do it with you." Then you role model expressing your feelings by having a little tantrum and yelling in your pillow. This teaches children how to label and express feelings in a healthy way.

It is important to get the angry energy out of our bodies before we communicate with those that we love. So many people come home from a stressful or frustrating day at work and then take out that stress on their family members. This is where the victim triangle can get triggered in a matter of minutes. Instead of dumping the intensity on your family, release the energy by having a tantrum, going to the gym or taking a nice relaxing bath. Then use clear, direct and loving language with family members. "When I left home this morning, you said you would have your homework done by tonight at six. It is now seven and the homework is still not finished. What I would like from you is for you to keep your agreements.

So please let me know when you are willing to keep the agreement to complete your homework." This type of a clear message uses no profanity, blame or shame, and does not in any way demean the other person. Therefore it is not abusive and is much more likely to receive a positive response than yelling and put downs are.

Healing through Emotions

The *Personal Transformation Intensive* is a group experience where it is safe to express feelings. People are taught the above principles and boundaries and groundrules are set. We have a clearing process that is used so that if someone gets triggered by someone else, we have a safe, structured way to deal with it. No one is allowed to take over the group or abuse anyone with their own "stuff." Just as in families, boundaries are very important in any group. This group experience is actually a role model for healthy families. It is the way to break out of the victim pattern and to create healthy families.

Unconditional Love

The concept of unconditional love is wonderfully healing to the child within. Most of us were loved with strings attached. The love was conditional based on performance and also based on if you were willing to play the family games. Unconditional love is given freely and without strings. This is where the real healing takes place in all of our therapeutic work.
When you can love the child within you, and he or she can feel the nurturing and the unconditional love, you will truly be healed.

How Do I Know When I Have Healed the Victim Triangle?

What we have seen is that victim consciousness seems to be very insidious. It's almost like a computer virus that seeps through many of your programs and may be invisible at first glance. As you begin to do the therapeutic work to "clean up" this victim virus, you begin to see changes in your life. This is most predominant in what or who you manifest in your life. An example is a young woman who used to come into my office and would always have a victim/ persecutor story to tell me. She would be upset over the jerk who tried to cut her car off on the freeway, or the one who moved in next door and was ruining her life. Each time I saw her we

139

would do work on these victim situations in her life. She then joined the Personal Transformation Intensive group where her victim issues were clearly brought to her attention. Through the group experience, she was finally able to see most clearly how she was attracting these situations into her life. She made a firm commitment to take her power in a healthy way and stop the victim/persecutor drama in her life.

She now more often has the experience of people slowing down to let her in when she is on the freeway rather than trying to cut her off. The man next door, who was ruining her life, recently brought her some soup to share and has volunteered to feed her cats when she is gone. What she is manifesting in her life is changing and she can feel the difference. The relationships she is attracting are no longer abusive, but actually feel much more loving and supportive. She is much more conscious of what and who she attracts into her life, and that she always has a choice.

There may be times when she slips back into a victim situation, but she now recognizes it sooner and is able to step away from it rather than to be sucked into it. She has literally changed her life for the better. And you can, too. It is time to take your power, make clear choices and discover who you really are.

Use the questionnaire on the following pages to become more clear about how feelings were dealt with in your childhood family, and how you deal with your emotions today.

How Were Feelings Dealt with in Your Childhood Family?

Anger
Shamed for expressing it, such as telling a boy he is a sissy or telling girls "That is not lady-like" or "Children should be seen and not heard."

or

Encouraged to express your feelings of anger, directly and openly.

Sadness-Tears
Punished for expressing it, such as "I'll give you something to cry about" or "Go to your room until you can stop."

or

Comforted and encouraged to explore the feelings to discover the causes.

Fear
Scared out of expressing feelings because of a rage-aholic or abusive parent.

or

Always taught that you have a right to feel your feelings, and that this is a safe world.

Others

How I Deal with Emotions

(Put appropriate number in box for each emotion listed below)

unhealthy responses
1. Hold it in
2. Numb emotions by using alcohol, pot, pills, food, the internet, nicotine, caffeine, shopping, television
3. Take it out on others
4. Somaticize (turn it into illness or pain)
5. Other _____

healthy responses
6. Verbal release (yell into hands or pillow)
7. Physical Release (exercise, chop wood, hit a pillow)
8. Cry
9. Communicate my feelings to the appropriate person in a non-abusive way
10. Other _____

	unhealthy	healthy
Anger	❑	❑
Hurt	❑	❑
Rejection	❑	❑
Sadness	❑	❑
Fear	❑	❑
Shame	❑	❑

AFFIRMATIONS
(write out one 25 times each day)

I accept all my emotions with love

I give myself permission to acknowledge my feelings

I release my emotions in healthy ways

I love and approve of myself

I release my stress with ease

I now choose physical activity as a way to release stress

I give myself permission to express my creativity

My body, mind and spirit are in complete harmony

Now, you write some of your own:

_____

_____

_____

_____

_____

_____

_____

Unconditional Love for Oneself and Others

Conditional Love   Unconditional Love

I will only love you if ...   I love who you *really* are

you change
you lose weight
you make more money
you look different
you act different
you fit into my image
    of husband/wife/son/daughter/boss
you impress my friends
you make me feel different
you do it the way I think it should be done
you produce
you perform

List those people that you love conditionally, and the conditions:

List those that you love unconditionally:

AFFIRMATIONS TO CHANGE
VICTIM/RESCUER PATTERNS

1. I now take back the power to make healthy choices in my life

2. I am 100% responsible for my experiences in my life

3. I am responsible for me, and only me

4. I now hold others able to solve their own problems

5. I now express my feelings in healthy ways

Directions: Choose which apply to you, or make up your own. Write out one affirmation 25 times each day to change *victim thinking*. Try writing some affirmations of your own.

_____

_____

_____

_____

_____

_____

_____

_____

_____

_____

Chapter 16
The Personal Transformation Intensive®

Self-love is not selfishness. Being selfish comes from feeling a lack or scarcity, and thus being afraid to give for fear of losing what little you have. The more love people feel for themselves, the more love they can give to others and the less selfish they are.

After a person has been in individual therapy for some time, a noticeable improvement will be seen. If both people in a couple are in treatment, the improvement will be greater still. I then most often recommend the *Personal Transformation Intensive®*. This experience does far more to change people's victim patterns than anything else I've experienced over my thirty years of doing therapeutic work!

This is a program of intensive weekends in a retreat setting which meets for five months. Some people choose to continue to more advanced levels or even to repeat the process several times. In the group, various processes are used to help group members clearly work through their individual and relationship issues. Processes include hypnotherapy, psychodrama, breathwork, meditation, and other group exercises designed to access and then directly express emotions. These processes are experiential rather than intellectual exercises; however, some cognitive teaching is also included.

Since so many people have numbed or denied their feelings, it is important for people to *feel*. At first they may not like the feelings, but most people soon learn to prefer *feelings* to dissociation and *numbness*. Then the feelings can be expressed and released, and real personal clarity ensues.

As the group progresses, each person's issues become crystal clear to him as well as to everyone else in the group. It becomes more and more difficult to go back to playing the old games. This is especially helpful in couples, where the problems are often located in the subconscious *projection*. Each person often projects his parental issues onto the other person, experiencing the spouse as "just like" one of his parents. Most people are not aware that they are doing this and they keep replaying these old patterns over and over again with each other. Through the group process, each person can now "own" what is his and stop the projection. This heals the relationship and ends the victim games.

147

Participants in the group may also be given assignments to do outside of the class, which help to illuminate their issues and offer opportunities to heal them. Participants are continually working to release their victim, codependent issues, and are diligently involved in their own healing process. They are taught to take responsibility for their own issues rather than blaming them on other people. We have many processes which help to accomplish this.

An important aspect of any group is that each person becomes a mirror for the others. The participants all begin to see reflections of themselves in each other. This is quite illuminating since we always see ourselves in others, and yet how many people walk around each day without the awareness that they are doing this?

One of the most valuable aspects of the group is the nurturing support that is available for each and every person. For many it is the first time that they have bared their souls to anyone. It is the first time that they have admitted to addictions, abuse or shame, sometimes even to themselves. When the truth is out and you realize that you are still loved, for some it is the first experience of unconditional love. This is the beginning of real self-esteem, and of true healing.

There are many other important aspects of the Intensive, but the most vital is the spiritual awakening which takes place. Most people, through the release of the false self and the reclaiming of the true self, have enlightenment experiences which they have never had before. These spiritual experiences include: a new sense of connection with one's Higher Power, however each person defines it to be; a revitalized connection with all aspects of one's self, including those child parts and inner resources left behind at times of trauma; and a newfound loving compassion for the significant relationships in one's life. This transformational process is personal growth by quantum leaps.

The *Personal Transformation Intensive*® (*PTI*) includes Heart-Centered Hypnotherapy, Energetic Psychodrama, Breathwork, the Clearing Process, Heart-Centered Meditation and Master Mind Groups. All of these processes are powerful tools for personal growth in and of themselves: however, in combination these dynamic tools become great catalysts for enlightenment and change. One young woman shared with me that before the *PTI* she had been depressed and suicidal all her life. All she could do was think about death and how she was going to kill herself. She finally bought a large gun and began carrying it around in her purse. She then bought bullets and loaded them into the gun with serious plans to pull the trigger. She enrolled in the *PTI* at the suggestion of a family member.

During the second meeting of the group, in her breathwork session, she had an amazing spiritual experience in which she realized what her true purpose for being here on earth is about and that her life did indeed have meaning. This one weekend changed the entire course of her life and it was at this point that she made a new decision to live. At the end of her *Personal Transformation Intensive*, she gave the gun away and truly is a transformed person. Her life is now unfolding in many new and exciting directions. She thanked me so much for developing this program which she said literally *saved her life*.

Breathwork and Rebirthing

There is more and more evidence that many of the problems in our lives, the lifelong dysfunctional patterns, go back to our birth or to experiences in the womb. For example, research now documents a clear connection between birth trauma and suicide attempts. There is a much higher risk of suicide and depression in people who have experienced birth trauma.[11]

I know this may seem incredible to you, especially if you have never experienced your birth. However, as you read the following accounts, you will understand how prenatal experience can affect us. First, it is necessary to understand that consciousness exists from the very moment of conception. Even though babies cannot talk, they certainly can hear, feel, and comprehend. In Chapter 11, I told you about Vicki, who regressed back to the womb where she knew intuitively that her parents didn't want her. She immediately felt rejected, and the internalized low self-esteem crippled her throughout her life. This is actually a common situation.

In hypnosis, a person can return to these experiences and feel them emotionally or watch them as if watching a movie. Sometimes in breathwork a person actually re-creates the physical sensation of the birth experience. Now, if this was traumatic, you may wonder why anyone would choose to experience it all over again. The reason is to heal it. Through rebirthing you can heal the birth traumas that may have been "clogging up" your life for years. The same techniques that are so effective in healing childhood traumas (for example, informing the child, or reframing, or re-parenting) work to heal birth and prenatal traumas.

In a breathwork session, Cynthia experienced feeling suffocated as she was going down the birth canal. She concluded from this that life is suffocating, and is a struggle for even the most basic needs (such as air). Once she adopted that belief, she began to make it happen in her life. As a child, she contracted asthma and allergy problems. Later, she became a smoker. She attracted people who would "hang on to her" and suffocate her in relationships. Life, especially relationships, always seemed like such a struggle.

Cynthia was able to reframe the birth experience later in the same session. The new birth experience was empowering, because she felt in control, exhilarated at being able to breathe deeply as she moved easily through the birth canal and out into the world. She reframed the experience not only in mental images but also physically so that her body had the actual visceral experience of unimpeded movement, and her lungs of filling with plentiful oxygen. Cynthia began rapid progress in resolving her struggles with getting her needs met at work and in personal relationships, and was successful in finally quitting smoking.

Once you go through the birth trauma, healing takes place because you go through it more consciously and with the perspective of your adult level of wisdom. To a newborn, struggling to survive and facing the unknown, going down the birth canal may seem like an eternity. With the dual awareness of infant and adult, you realize that you have resources and choices now that you did not have then, and that you do not need to re-create the original experience in your life any more.

Rebirthing, through hypnotherapy or breathwork, is an "enlightenment" process; people gain new heights of clarity about their lives. For example, I recently worked with a man who has been a victim and a rescuer for much of his life. We'll call him Barry. He has felt helpless with drugs and alcohol in his life, and has had very dissatisfying relationships in his life with women. The pattern has been that he finds victim women and rescues them. They then become so dependent on him that he feels suffocated and wants to "get out." But he then feels guilty about hurting them, so he stays. He uses a lot of drugs to "anesthetize" the guilt.

In a hot tub rebirthing session, Barry started rocking back and forth, banging his head against the edge of the tub. Then he would stop and cry and curl up in a ball and withdraw. His feeling was that he was trying to "get out," but it was causing his mother pain. She was closing her legs and holding him back. Every time Barry tried to get out, he felt guilty because he felt responsible for his mother's pain. He would then stop trying and "go unconscious" from the anesthetic in his mother's body.

Barry's relationship with his mother all during his life was merely a re-creation of his birth. His mother developed a dependency on Barry, making him responsible for her happiness. He became her rescuer, and accepted the position of being responsible for her. She became very overprotective and would not "let go" of him; as he grew, he felt suffocated. He did not have the freedom that some of the other kids had.

As Barry got older, he began to become interested in girls; his mother was very threatened by this. The tighter she held on, the harder he fought to get away from her and the more guilt he felt. His mother used guilt to try to control and manipulate him. The more guilt he felt, the more he resented her. Of course, he could not express the resentment, so he held it in. The resentment grew and so he began to use the common anesthetics in our culture: cigarettes, drugs and alcohol. As a teenager, he began repressing his guilt and resentment with the use of these substances.

The relationships in his life tended to follow the same patterns. Barry would attract a dependent woman and then develop mutual dependency. He would always play the role of the rescuer. As the woman began to suffocate him, he would feel trapped and try to "push out." This would, of course, cause her pain and so she would "hold on tighter" to try to stop the pain. Just as it doesn't work in childbirth, it doesn't work in relationships. And so the harder she holds on, the more he tries to get out and the more guilt he feels. The more guilt anyone feels, the more resentment there is. And for Barry, as for many people, the more resentment he feels, the more drugs he uses.

Through rebirthing and the Intensive group experience, Barry was able to discover this pattern and heal it. But it cannot be healed on the conscious level. An experience of rebirthing, somatically and emotionally returning to the original traumatic experience, is necessary in order to accomplish this level of healing. His relationships with women are much healthier now. He is attracting women who are winners instead of needy victims. He does not need to attract suffocation or guilt into his life. He also does not need to re-create resentment which would have led him back into using drugs and alcohol.

Barry's healing process took about a year using the Intensive group process. If this healing could have been accomplished with an intellectual process (and I doubt that it could), it might have taken anywhere from three to ten years.

Many people, through rebirthing, get in touch with the awareness that they were not wanted. Perhaps the mother was a teenager who was not ready for the responsibility of a child. The mother may have already had three or more children and the pregnancy may have been an accident. Perhaps the family was not financially ready for another baby. There are many reasons why parents at some point in their lives do not want a child. And yet for whatever reason, the child may be born anyway.

A person who was unwanted at birth will go through life with the rejection pattern. In an effort to "heal" the feeling of rejection, this person will re-create one relationship after another like that of the original relationship with the parent. Through rebirthing in hypnotherapy or breathwork and the group Intensive experience, the individual can actually eliminate the need to attract rejection into his life.

Persons who attract rejection into their lives are definitely involved in the victim triangle. They feel helpless to attract anything other than rejection. They will inevitably attract a persecutor who persecutes through withdrawal of love. Then the victim gets to feel victimized all over again.

Many victim patterns are already established in the family long before the child is born. It may go back generations upon generations. Awareness of the situation certainly helps, but it does not change the old patterns. The Personal Transformation Intensive process reaches down to the depths of the old patterns and weeds them out, allowing new healthy patterns to grow.

Energetic Psychodrama

Judith has had a life long problem of feeling like a fake. Even though she is a well- established professional with twenty years of experience in her field, she never feels confident about her skills or her ability to attract clients. She has done years of counseling and therapy and yet has continued to feel like an "imposter." She also has had difficulty finding a spiritual connection.

We began her psychodrama on these issues and she was immediately catapulted back to being eight years old and terrified. She was in the Baptist church and her Sunday School teacher was insisting that she had to be Baptized because she might be run over by a car today when she left church and then she would immediately go to Hell. The other church members, including her parents, were all saying the same thing and trying to get her and her best friend to be baptized. They were saying that all little children were sinners and even babies were born "in sin," and that "Everyone was going to Hell unless they were baptized."

As in all of our psychodramas, group members play roles for the main character, so group members were playing the roles of her parents, her Sunday School teacher and the church members who were terrifying her with the religious dogma. The little eight-year-old Judith was filled with fear that she might be run over by a car and go to Hell. So she decided to be baptized, even though she felt unworthy to be baptized, didn't really understand what it was and didn't really want to do it in the first place.

In the psychodrama, we walked her through this powerful experience, with someone playing her Sunday School teacher yelling at her (which she had pre-scripted), "Now you know you're a sinner, don't you?" In re-living this momentous childhood experience, Judith realized that it was in this very experience where her feeling of being an imposter had begun. Terrified, she had lied and said "yes" she was a sinner, when she didn't believe that at all. She believed that children were good and she believed that God loved all children. So in being baptized she felt she lied, and that she betrayed her true belief in God. This incident has caused her to feel very disconnected from God for the next fifty years of her life.

In psychodrama, as in all the work that we do, we always build in a *corrective experience*.[12] This emotional correction allows the individual to re-experience the old, unresolved conflict *but with a new empowered ending*. In her corrective experience, Judith pushed all these Baptist church people out of her life and told them the truth about her beliefs about God. She expressed that her God is loving and that all children are born in love not in sin. She was able to truly take her power and speak her truth in the regressed ego state of her little eight-year-old, which in turn was powerfully healing for her adult.

Judith has had a major transformation from the work that she did in this psychodrama session. She has attracted more clients in her profession since she no longer feels like an imposter. She truly values herself and the work she does. She now has a clear and fulfilling spiritual connection.

As in all psychodramas, the roles played by other group members often trigger feelings for them or other observers. That in turn often leads to a psychodrama for the next person. Judith's highly charged work certainly triggered many people's memories of their own religious traumas as children. The woman who played the role of the Sunday School teacher pointedly recalled the religious dogma in her childhood church and the devastating effect it had on her for many years. She was then able to retrieve memories that had been repressed for forty years, complete her psychodrama, and reclaim her true relationship with her spirituality and her concept of God. This demonstrates the profound healing power of psychodrama. She was truly grateful for the opportunity to play the role for Judith, and then to get her own healing in return.

Another very moving psychodrama was played out by Fred. He states that he has difficulty maintaining intimate relationships with women in his

153

life. Most of his relationships don't last more than a few months and usually end up with the woman admonishing, "Let's just be friends." He is a man in his late forties and is feeling very discouraged and lonely by this lack of intimacy in his life. He is very aware of an actual fear or anxiety in his stomach that comes up when he gets into a relationship with a woman: the fear of rejection. He also has had many financial problems and worries about money, which intensify when he is in relationship with a woman.

As his psychodrama began, he soon regressed to an experience as a six-year-old, alone in his room listening to his parents fighting. His father was yelling at his mother for spending too much money. He kept saying, "We don't have a pot to piss in and you're spending too much money." Then he began accusing her of having sex with another man. The mother began screaming back defending herself and then crying hysterically.

Little Freddie felt helpless in his room to get their attention or to be noticed at all. He was there night after night listening to the same fights over and over again. He was lonely and all he had was his toys and his dog. He would cuddle up with his dog to try to feel some comfort. Then his father would come into his room and start yelling at him, "Get this damn dog out of the house." The father pulled the dog out of Freddie's room and threw it out into the yard. Freddie concluded, "My needs will never be met. I'll always be alone. I'll just hide."

There were several kids in the neighborhood (played by group members) who wanted to play with Freddie. He wanted to play, too, but didn't really know how. He felt unsure of himself and feared being rejected. Whenever the kids reached out to him, he could feel that fear coming up in his stomach, that same fear of rejection that comes up currently when he gets into a relationship. Then his father would come out and make him come home, "Freddie, get back in this house." He knew that he wasn't allowed to make friends or get too close or let friends come over. He knew that he wouldn't want any friends to come over and hear his parents fighting. Even at this young age of six, his very clear decision was, "It is safer to be alone!"

Through the thousands of regressions I have witnessed, I have discovered that children of every age draw *conclusions* about themselves, and then make *decisions* about how to behave based on those conclusions.[13] This seems to be universally true and is what I call the unconscious programming that governs much of our behavior. Those childhood conclusions and decisions have immense impact for a lifetime, because they are, first of all, accepted to define one's very worth and identity. In addition, because they came to be at the time of early traumatic experience, they are deeply embedded within the individual's "world view," as an unchallenged "fact of life." Through regression tools such as Heart-Centered hypnotherapy, psychodrama and breathwork, we can go back and discover what conclusions we have drawn about ourselves and what decisions are still affecting our behavior. Until these conclusions and decisions are brought to conscious awareness and explicitly changed, they still govern our lives, even though they may have been made when we were six years old! My experience is that many of these early conclusions and decisions were, in fact, made much earlier, as a toddler, in infancy, or even as a prenate in the womb.

As we began the corrective phase of Fred's psychodrama, we "grew him up" and had him reclaim his power so that he could speak his truth to his parents. He was able to express his deep grief and profound anger about the total lack of role modeling for a healthy relationship in their family. He expressed outrage and a deep sense of hopelessness that they had never taught him how to have intimacy, and that in fact the only closeness he had, with his dog, was even ripped away from him. Once Fred had "grown up" in the psychodrama, he felt gut-wrenching compassion for the little boy. He was able to speak with his six-year-old, now played by another group member, and help him develop a new conclusion about connection with others being safe and fulfilling. He created new decisions to replace the old decision to hide and isolate. He also saw where all his fears about money came from.

Fred has made some major changes in his life from this psychodrama experience. He has realized that the fear of rejection and the old decision that it was safer to be alone have caused him to continually cut off relationships before they had a chance to begin. He is now allowing relationships to take their course, to go slow and really give them a chance to blossom and grow. He has also realized that his father's repeated words, "We don't have a pot to piss in" was a belief that he had accepted unconsciously for himself. He has turned that around and now has an abundant flow of resources in his life. He is very grateful for the personal healing work and continues to do it since he has acknowledged this is just the beginning for him.

The Master Mind Process

The Master Mind process is an ancient formula for success through collaboration among like-minded people. Napoleon Hill popularized the process in his book *Think and Grow Rich*. Hill was commissioned by the

155

steel magnate Andrew Carnegie to interview over 500 of America's successful men, including Henry Ford, John D. Rockefeller and Thomas Edison, to find a success formula that could be used by the average person. Twenty years later Hill published his book *Think and Grow Rich*. This book identified thirteen principles of success, one of which is the Power of the Master Mind. He said, "A goal is a dream with a deadline;" "If you do not conquer *self*, you will be conquered *by self*;" and "You must get involved to have an impact. No one is impressed with the won-lost record of the referee." Most well-known is his quote: "Whatever the Mind of man can *conceive* and *believe* it can *achieve*."

Master Minding is a powerful method of getting clear about your goals, both short-term, "What should I be doing now?" and long-term, "What do I want to achieve in my life?" We may even delve into more profound issues such as "What is my purpose for being here on earth?" We have processes that we employ in our Personal Transformation Intensive groups which help people to get clear on these issues. You cannot set goals if you first and foremost are not clear about what you want. We have discovered that many people just wander through their lives without making clear choices or knowing what their path is. Most people grow up, get married, have kids, get a job, change jobs, but how many of these were really clear conscious choices? That is why people fall so hard when the mid-life crisis comes along. Between the ages of thirty and forty, people often begin to feel restless, unhappy and maybe even have an affair to medicate these feelings. It is usually because we haven't truly been taught to get clear about what we want in our lives, what experiences we are looking for and what brings us joy and fulfillment, and then encouraged to pursue it.

A Master Mind group consists of people who work together in harmony to achieve diverse goals. That is, they each are working toward their own goals, but are also supporting each of the other group members to work toward *their* own goals. Each draws something from the others, and each contributes freely to the others in the group. When many minds concentrate together, the activity generates a power over and above the sum total of each of the individual minds, as though an invisible force joins the group.

The process of just setting an intention, witnessed and supported by others, sets in motion the fulfillment of that intention. No one has said that truth better than the German poet/ philosopher Goethe:

Until one is committed, there is hesitancy, the chance to draw back, always ineffectiveness. Concerning all acts of initiative (and creation), there is one elementary truth the ignorance of which kills countless ideas and splendid plans: that the moment one definitely commits oneself, then providence moves too.
All sorts of things occur to help one that would never otherwise have occurred. A whole stream of events issues from the decision, raising in one's favor all manner of unforeseen incidents and meetings and material assistance, which no man could have dreamed would have come his way.
Whatever you can do or dream you can, begin, boldness has genius, power and magic in it.
Begin it now.

Years ago, I set the goal in my Master Mind group of being invited to travel to three foreign countries that needed healing to teach Heart-Centered Hypnotherapy to professional therapists. I had no idea which countries it would be or how it would come to be. Within two years I had been sought out by the government of Kuwait, a university in Taiwan, and a professional association in South Africa. How gratifying those invitations were to me, and how immensely grateful I am for the opportunity to collaborate with the wonderful people I have come to know in those countries. The Master Mind process had once again truly worked!

People in our *PTI* groups nearly always find their Master Mind group experience to be valuable. People who have had a home for sale languishing on the market, as soon as they included the sale in their Master Mind process, the home almost sold overnight. And they usually got more than their asking price! Many people in Master Mind groups have literally doubled and tripled their incomes by using the process. We have had people attract the type of relationships they have longed for but never thought they could find. One woman named Loretta was sitting with us at the dining room table as we did the Master Mind process for relationships with her. The process includes carefully visualizing each of the characteristics and qualities that you want in the mate you are looking for. There happened to be a training group at our house that weekend. Not more than five minutes later a man that Loretta had known from one of the groups came walking through the door and asked her if she would like to take a walk with him. Their relationship progressed from that day forward. Even though she had known him previously, she had never seen him through "those eyes" until we did the Master Mind process. They are now living and working together in perfect harmony and both seem to be the perfect mate for the other.

There is an important reason why we include the Master Mind process in all of the work that we do in healing the victim triangle. As we have discussed, the Victim is the person or part of you who feels powerless and blames others for every problem. When you get clear on what you want in your life and make clear choices, there is no one to blame. Master Minding is a direct way to take back your personal power in your life and release the victim consciousness. If a choice that you have made does not work out for you, see it as a learning experience and bring it back to your Master Mind group and re-work it. The Victim can be very insidious and will then try to say, "Well, I have no one *to blame* but myself." Even if you are blaming yourself, you are still in the victim consciousness. Take the word *blame* out of your vocabulary and change it to *responsibility*. The Master Mind process is a way to learn to take full responsibility for your choices in your life and to finally release the Victim.

Meditation

We utilize group meditation to begin every morning of every group meeting in the *PTI*. By doing so, we all harmonize our energies, we quiet the mind from its usual constant chatter, and we set a common direction with each other for the coming day. Several elements are important to include in these meditations. One is to sit in a circle, holding hands. This facilitates the effortless flow of our energies. Another is to acknowledge all of the spiritual connections or forms of worship that various people may relate to: God/Goddess, Jesus, Buddha, Allah, Yahweh, Great Spirit, the Creator, the Divine Mother, Higher Power, White Light, Mother Earth, etc. People of every tradition are made to feel totally welcome in the circle. Each person is meditating quietly and we honor and respect each person's individuality and personal beliefs. The focus is on opening up the heart center to unconditional love and creating a space of internal peace.

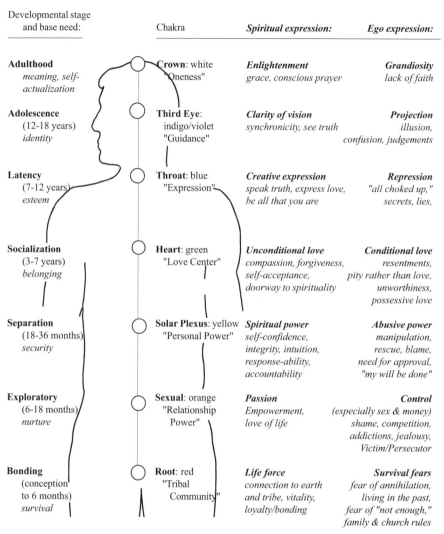

Developmental stage and base need:	Chakra	*Spiritual expression:*	*Ego expression:*
Adulthood *meaning, self-actualization*	**Crown**: white "Oneness"	*Enlightenment* grace, conscious prayer	*Grandiosity* lack of faith
Adolescence (12-18 years) *identity*	**Third Eye**: indigo/violet "Guidance"	*Clarity of vision* synchronicity, see truth	*Projection* illusion, confusion, judgements
Latency (7-12 years) *esteem*	**Throat**: blue "Expression"	*Creative expression* speak truth, express love, be all that you are	*Repression* "all choked up," secrets, lies,
Socialization (3-7 years) *belonging*	**Heart**: green "Love Center"	*Unconditional love* compassion, forgiveness, self-acceptance, doorway to spirituality	*Conditional love* resentments, pity rather than love, unworthiness, possessive love
Separation (18-36 months) *security*	**Solar Plexus**: yellow "Personal Power"	*Spiritual power* self-confidence, integrity, intuition, response-ability, accountability	*Abusive power* manipulation, rescue, blame, need for approval, "my will be done"
Exploratory (6-18 months) *nurture*	**Sexual**: orange "Relationship Power"	*Passion* Empowerment, love of life	*Control* (especially sex & money) shame, competition, addictions, jealousy, Victim/Persecutor
Bonding (conception to 6 months) *survival*	**Root**: red "Tribal Community"	*Life force* connection to earth and tribe, vitality, loyalty/bonding	*Survival fears* fear of annihilation, living in the past, fear of "not enough," family & church rules

Personal Transformation Chart

The Chakras or Energy Centers

Chakra is the Sanskrit word for wheel. There are seven major energy wheels or chakras in the body, located along the spinal column. This is a very ancient and fascinating teaching that I studied in India forty years ago and continue to learn about.

**When the Chakras are dissonant,
the body signals us with symptoms of dis-ease.**

**When the Chakras are activated in harmony,
the Endocrine System creates Immunity from dis-ease.**

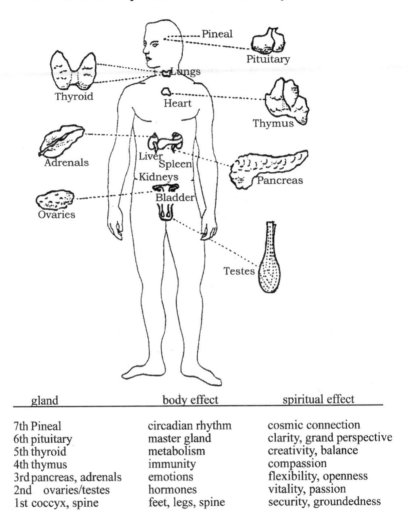

gland	body effect	spiritual effect
7th Pineal	circadian rhythm	cosmic connection
6th pituitary	master gland	clarity, grand perspective
5th thyroid	metabolism	creativity, balance
4th thymus	immunity	compassion
3rd pancreas, adrenals	emotions	flexibility, openness
2nd ovaries/testes	hormones	vitality, passion
1st coccyx, spine	feet, legs, spine	security, groundedness

The way that we practice this meditation is to bring the attention to and open up each of the chakra centers. We instruct people to breathe into and out of each chakra as if they had a nose there. This really creates the

160

feeling of openness and allows the energy to flow through each chakra. We work up from the base of the spine to the top of the head and visualize a fountain of energy moving up our spines. This opens up the energy into the spinal column and actually produces much more energy for the entire body. Energy can get blocked easily in the spine and chakras from stress, emotions and accidents. It can also get blocked from what we call ego issues or emotions such as fear, shame, guilt, unresolved grief and rage (which is years of unexpressed anger). This meditation can begin to remove those blockages and heal those old injuries. People are often amazed when they discover how much more energy they have from doing these meditations.

The first chakra, or *Root Chakra*, lies at the base of your spine and, through meditating on this chakra, you help yourself become more grounded, more solid and much more powerful at the physical levels of your life. It is also the area where people have located their fears of not having enough or not having their needs met. Do you often hear yourself saying, "I don't have enough time, money, love, sex, etc?" If this is an issue for you, then you may have root chakra work to do. This meditation may be the way to begin.

The second, or *Sexual Chakra*, is located in the sexual organs, and is related not only to sexual and sensual passion, but also to a much more general passion for life: spiritual vitality. The ego issues located here have to do with control versus spontaneity. If you find yourself always trying to control people and situations, then this may be the place for you to meditate. People who have been sexually abused may have blockages in this chakra.

The third chakra is called the *Power Chakra*, and is associated with fire, with combustion, with personal power, joy, and integrity. It is located between the navel and the solar plexus, and represents a "fire in the belly." It is the chakra where much of the victim triangle plays out. This is because it is the power center. If you were overpowered as a child or as an adult, or find yourself in power struggles with others, then this may be the chakra which needs to be opened for you.

The fourth chakra, the *Heart Chakra*, is located in the center of the chest, equidistant between the first and the seventh chakras, between earth and heaven. It balances the chakras above with the chakras below, through its potential for unconditional love. What most blocks the heart center from realizing this potential of love is low self-esteem or feeling unworthy of love and acceptance. Also, unresolved grief and resentment can cause

161

energy blockages here. If you feel empty inside and a lack of love, this may be where your work needs to begin.

The fifth chakra, called the *Throat Chakra*, is located in our throat region, and is the center of creativity, communication, and of expressing the depths of our true self. This chakra often gets blocked by fear and shame. As children we are told to be seen but not heard. We are often told to be quiet and to keep the family secrets. The core of shame runs so deep that many people have great blockages about expressing their true feelings, telling their truth, or becoming who they truly are meant to be. They have identified with their *false self*. If this resonates with you, then this may be an area for you to meditate and work on.

The *Third Eye Chakra* is the sixth chakra, located between and just above your eyes on the forehead. It is the seat of true wisdom, where your thinking mind comes into contact with your intuitive mind. This is where, when you listen during meditation, your Higher Self speaks to you directly and where you experience your visionary self. The third eye is about having true clarity in your life instead of feeling confused, judgmental or overwhelmed. When clarity comes to your third eye energy center, you feel the peace of mind that comes with *knowing* intuitively. If confusion and judgment trouble you, then perhaps the third eye is a place for you to focus.

Called the *Crown Chakra*, the seventh chakra is located at the top of the head, and is the intersection of your earthly being and all that lies above and beyond. It is the place where you can release ego attachments and become one with all that is in the universe, or grasp onto ego attachments with grandiosity and think that you are the center of the universe. This is the place where that fountain of energy can flow right up from the base of your spine, opening up the spinal column and all the chakras in an amazing light show.

If you have energy blocked in these areas, which most people do, it is important to do the psychological as well as spiritual work to unblock them. People who have had blocked energy for years, or who have traumatic memories, may begin to have illness or dis-ease in these areas of their bodies. Notice when your energy is low and you get sick, what areas of your body are usually affected and which chakra is closest to that area. This will give you some clues to the emotional work that you may need to do in order to heal. See the Personal Transformation Chart on page 159.

The lower chakras all have victim energy connected to them. If you are stuck in the first chakra, you often feel like your needs aren't met and you don't have enough of what you need in your life. This creates the victim energy of feeling powerless. You may stuff yourself with food, cigarettes or alcohol to try to push down or numb those feelings. And you then probably blame (persecute) those closest to you for not meeting your needs. This blaming/persecuting, of course, pushes those that you love even further away from you. Then, feeling lonely and rejected, you move right back into the victim feelings and become trapped in that triangle again.

If you are stuck in the second chakra, you usually try to control others around you, especially regarding when, where and how to have sex. This may go back to being sexually abused as a child and feeling like a victim. When you try to control things now in order to feel safe, you often come across as a rescuer or persecutor. Money is another major area where you may try to control things, often unsuccessfully. You may try to control your spouse's spending and become a persecutor, or you may feel like a victim when you can't even control your own. You may use money to rescue others and then end up resenting it, only to blame/persecute them! Money is such a loaded issue for most people, and is often the straw that breaks the camel's back when a marriage is teetering on the brink of divorce. It may be difficult for you to live in the moment and be spontaneous because your fears and anxiety increase when you are not in control. If you tend to have physical problems in this area such as infections or blockages or pain, this is another clue that emotional work needs to be done here.

The third chakra is really where most of the victim drama is played out because it is the power chakra, and as we have discussed throughout this book, the victim drama is about feeling powerless in your life. The third chakra is also about expressing emotions. If you have been blocked in expressing your true feelings to those closest to you in your life, it would certainly keep you from feeling powerful. You may have had authority struggles in your life with, for example, abusive church teachers, abusive parents or inconsistent authority figures. Power struggles certainly develop from growing up with, for example, nuns bashing children's heads into the blackboard for giving the wrong answers, priests sexually molesting children in the rectory, or your father beating you with a belt at your mother's request. And usually, of course, children were not allowed to express any feelings about the abuse that was happening. Some people may not even remember their abuse. The power of healing in a group is that when one person heals, it opens up the healing opportunities for all the other group members.

Between the second and third chakra are located many organs.

163

As we do the awakening work in lower chakras, the upper, spiritual chakras open. The heart chakra is the doorway to the spiritual centers. We know that the most powerful spiritual experiences come when people have done their emotional work to heal the victim issues in their lower chakras. In our six-day Heart-Centered hypnotherapy training program, I have worked with hundreds of people who have never had any spiritual connections or experiences in their lives. Many don't even know what I mean when I speak of a spiritual experience. As they do the Heart-Centered hypnotherapy and the meditations, each day they became more and more aware. After only two hypnotherapy sessions and a few days of group meditation, most people have powerful, life-changing spiritual awakenings.

We always invite participants in the circle meditation to visualize bringing into the circle anyone they want to share the healing power with. Each person can call out those individuals' names, inviting them to receive healing energy. Often, particular people will come to mind for people in the circle, perhaps someone who their conscious mind would not have thought of. The energy of the shared invitation draws those in need like a powerful magnet. The sacredness of the experience also brings amazing closeness and bonding to the group members.

Another principle is to ask each person in the meditation circle to bring to awareness their own individual spiritual connection, to acknowledge the presence in the room of all the angels, masters, messengers, and divine beings who offer spiritual support. This is done silently and is a method to make us aware of all the helpers that we do have. It is also reminding us that each individual path is honored. It is important to remember to say "Thank you" and feel gratitude for all the many blessings we receive each and every day.

How it all Works Together

Remember Napoleon Hill's statement: "Whatever the Mind of man can *conceive* and *believe* it can *achieve*." The hypnotherapy, psychodrama, breathwork, and meditation in a *PTI* program work together seamlessly to facilitate people's stepping into their highest potential. One must heal the old beliefs of unworthiness and limitation before opening to the grand possibilities that lie ahead for each one of us. The opening takes place on several levels. Rigid, repressed or chaotic emotions are unlocked, acknowledged, expressed and released. The sense of identity itself is liberated from the tyrants of self-blame, unrealistic self-expectations, and dependency. Through the somatic components of these healing techniques, especially the breathwork, the fearful reflex reactions and traumatic memories embedded deep within the body are resolved physically and released. Only then can the new insights and beliefs be incorporated into the body's nervous system and structure. And the meditation allows one to create a balance between the sacredness of life and the groundedness of effective action.

I'd like to share with you a letter sent to me recently, one of hundreds that I am blessed to receive each year. They remind me that the people whose lives I am honored to touch are in turn touching others in an ever-growing circle of healing. I am confident that I am fulfilling my purpose in this life, and I am full of humility and gratitude.

Dear Diane and David,

The Miracle is not to walk on water, the miracle is to walk on the green earth, dwelling deeply in the present moment and feeling truly alive. You have each in your own unique ways, offered me the opportunity to walk on the earth with love, dignity and honor. You have gifted me with the chance to find, touch, explore, savor, understand and honor my own true self and all its mysteries and wonders.

Diane, thank you for your unending teachings, commitment, and dedication to helping all of us search for and discover ways to become healed and whole. You have opened so many doors for all of your students, some of which, like mine, were deadbolted shut! And you have guided us into a world of safety, trust, clarity, understanding and finally freedom!

Where my path will lead me next, is only known to God, but I know that I carry both of your healing messages within me. I know and believe that I will use them to help others as you have helped me. This is my dearest wish and dream. I honor and bless each of you.

In loving gratitude for the healing work you do...

Your student

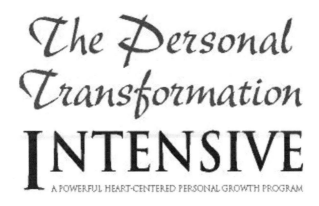

A POWERFUL HEART-CENTERED PERSONAL GROWTH PROGRAM

If you are interested in more information about the PTI program, or would like to locate a scheduled PTI near you, please go to this website:

www.PTIntensive.com

and follow the link

Endnotes

[1] (page 6) The conceptualizations of the Victim Trap, with Victim, Rescuer, and Persecutor roles, derives from Eric Berne. In his seminal book *Games People Play* (1964), Berne first elucidated his conceptualization of interactional roles between people as "Games." While he identified many different Games, one included the roles of "victim," "persecutor" and "rescuer." It was the Alcoholic Game (pages 73-81). He clearly describes with many examples how people in relationship with each other can shift from one role to another, from persecutor to rescuer, for example, and back again. I have adapted this conceptualization to explain a wide variety of dysfunctional codependent relationships.

The graphical representation of it as a triangle was first proposed by Stephen Karpman (1968), calling it the "drama triangle." Ruppert & Ziff (1994), following the terminology initiated in this book (1989), refer to the "Persecutor/Rescuer/Victim Triangle."

Holloway (1977) states the following:

> "The Hurtful Adapted Child, Helpful Adapted Child, and Helpless Adapted Child are early prototypes for the roles respectively of Persecutor, Rescuer, and Victim initially described by Berne in the Life Game, *Alcoholic*, and later elaborated by Karpman in the development of the drama triangle."

[2] (page 24) Research with infants and their mothers shows that even the healthiest and most attuned mother misses or misinterprets her infant's signals some of the time. These moments of dyssynchrony are normal and healthy if they are immediately followed by the mother repairing her misunderstanding, bringing the momentary conflict into resolution. If the mother is not able to understand what her baby is communicating, then the infant or young child takes on the burdensome responsibility for repairing dyssynchronies (Pound, 1982). These children then become predisposed to overdeveloped empathy and concern for others, as well as guilt and shame (Zahn-Waxler & Radke-Yarrow, 1990). Thus the child develops a hypervigilance for cues from others, and a style of relating that Bowlby (1980) referred to as "compulsive caregiving." The child's vigilance to the subjective experience of others may lead to neglect or invalidation of her own subjective experience and the tendency to rely on external confirmation to maintain self-esteem and the sense of identity (de Groot & Rodin, 1994). This child grows up to be a full-blown rescuer.

Incidentally, research has shown a widespread gender difference in mother-infant interactions. In general, sons experience less dyssynchrony in their interactions with their mothers than daughters do (Biringen et al., 1994; Robinson et al., 1993; Robinson & Biringen, 1995). Mothers exhibit greater matching of infant sons' affect (e.g., the mother smiling at a smiling infant or showing sadness to a sad infant), while maternal sensitivity with infant daughters is associated with the *infant* responsible for matching the *mothers'* affect. In other words, sons are engaged in more child-directed interactions, and daughters are more engaged in mother-directed interactions. This common pattern explains gender differences that appear as children grow into adults.

3 (page 62) Learned helplessness. We define learned helplessness as a conditioned denial of one's ability to impact his/her environment. Children learn to accept their helplessness when it is reinforced by significant caregivers ("You can't do that," or "That is too hard for you to do"). We define powerlessness as a generalized helplessness, added to the need for an outside force to intercede (Abramson et al, 1978). Children are taught by a rescuing parent, for example, that not only are they incapable of doing some particular task, but that they need the parent to do it for them. In this way, helplessness becomes powerlessness, and treatment becomes very difficult.

4 (page 70) One way of describing the phenomenon of ego states is that one becomes *absorbed* in a particular state, for example watching a movie or reading a story, arguing with one's spouse or lecturing one's children, focusing on one's weight or on the satisfaction of a compulsive desire. Absorption, or confining one's attention to narrow segments of reality, is a state of trance, and is therefore highly suggestible. If one becomes chronically absorbed in an identity ("dumb blonde" or "adaptive child" or "rage-aholic") then one is locked into a highly limited repertoire of behaviors.

Ego state therapy is a therapeutic approach which recognizes that every individual incorporates numerous discreet ego states, with boundaries ranging from non-flexible to highly permeable, making up a "family of self" (Watkins & Watkins, 1982). Each of these ego states is a part of one's personality with a unique historical development, a particular set of thoughts and feelings and beliefs. From moment to moment, the individual dissociates from one ego state into another ego state. Some ego states are dysfunctional, or maladaptive, in that they choose behaviors which are not in the highest good of the individual. The strategy of therapeutic change is not to eliminate maladaptive ego states, but rather to encourage such an ego state to become more adaptive, to make behavior choices more congruent with the person's overall benefit.

5 (page 74) The term "disowned parts" is from Berne. It represents basically the same concept as "shadow part" in Jungian terminology: aspects of oneself that were repressed as too bad (unacceptable) or too good (unattainable).

6 (page 74) Rossi and Cheek (1988) explain in great detail the way in which state-dependent memory is activated through clinical hypnosis and other trance states to access and heal early trauma. Following traumatic events, details of the incident that were vivid when it took place become vague and more or less forgotten. This is because the special stress-released information substances that encoded their traumatic memories have changed as their mind-body returned to normal. The memories are thus not available to normal consciousness, and the phenomenon is called traumatic amnesia. The traumatic memories are still present and active, and they may influence the trauma victim's dreams and/or be expressed as psychosomatic symptoms. The memories are *dissociated* from normal consciousness and encoded on deeply imprinted physiological levels where they form the nuclei of psychosomatic and psychological problems. The severity of these problems depends on the age of the person, the degree to which the traumatic situation is acknowledged and reviewed within oneself or with others, the type of emotional support received, and the degree to which they are insidious. *Insidious trauma* (Root, 1992) is pervasive in one's experience, i.e., characterized by repetitive and cumulative experiences of oppression, violence, genocide, or femicide. Unlike traumatic events that intrude on an otherwise benign life experience, insidious traumas create and reinforce assumptions that life itself is unsafe. They assault every level of security a person has: physical, psychological, interpersonal, and spiritual (Zimberoff & Hartman, 1998).

7 (page 75) The term "false self" was introduced by British psychoanalyst Donald Winnicott (1960). If the child is repeatedly interrupted in self-directed experiences by a demanding caregiver, he/she becomes prematurely and compulsively attuned to the demands of others. This child loses awareness of its own spontaneous needs and develops a false sense of self based on compliance and performance.

8 (page 78) By the first three years of life, personalities are already largely formed. "Early conclusions" or "internal working models" are the basic deeply embedded beliefs about self and the world formed from the earliest

experiences, which then are carried forward in time as templates for how one sees the world and functions in it.

> Starting, we may suppose, towards the end of his first year, and probably especially actively during his second and third when he acquires the powerful and extraordinary gift of language, a child is busy constructing working models of how the physical world may be expected to behave, how his mother and other significant persons may be expected to behave, how he himself may be expected to behave, and how each interacts with the other. Within the framework of these working models he evaluates his situation and makes his plans. And within the framework of the working models of his mother and himself he evaluates special aspects of his situation and makes his attachment plans (Bowlby, 1969/1982, p. 354).

9 (page 106) The hypnobehavioral approach to psychotherapy means working directly to alleviate the client's neurotic or dysfunctional symptoms within the trance state, i.e., integrating hypnosis with behavior modification or behavior therapy techniques. Addressing many of these techniques directly to the unconscious rather than to the cognitive mind, as in conventional behavior modification, can be much more powerful as a change agent. It is our experience and belief that hypnobehavioral techniques contribute the most to effective therapy when they are combined with deeper psychodynamic (age regression and cathartic) experience rather than being the sole focus of the session. Behavior modification techniques are much more effective when used in experiential therapy than within the cognitive verbal approach. That is, we find real limitations in simply placing a person into a trance state, providing behavior modification techniques and related suggestions, and then waking the client from the trance. Changing a behavior pattern works most effectively when behavior therapy techniques are applied to the client's ego state most closely associated with the behavior needing to be changed. Examples include: *extinguishing* an unwanted symptom, a form of systematic desensitization; *modeling*, or social reinforcement, to induce a subject to imitate a constructive behavior so that it can be further positively reinforced; *anchoring*, which associates a feeling of being powerful with a mental or visual image which represents a desired behavioral outcome for the client; and *behavioral rehearsal*, which allows a person to try out and practice a desired but unfamiliar behavior (e.g., assertiveness).

10 (page 113) *Super-responsibility.* Some people learn early that if their needs are going to be met, they must be the one to meet them. In fact, they may extrapolate that if *anyone*'s needs in their home are going to be met, they must be the one to do so. Such a person automatically assumes responsibility for everything, believing that no one else is trustworthy or

170

capable of accomplishing the task. Rather than living one's own life fully, this individual over-commits, performing as "building superintendent" in every situation. The exaggerated sense of responsibility usually derives from 'parentification,' defined as an on-going family interactional pattern in which a child is excessively and inappropriately assigned roles and responsibilities normally reserved for adults, i.e., taking care of adults and/or siblings. Parentification requires a premature identification with the parent(s)' expectations and needs, at the expense of the development of the child's true talents and gifts, often leaving the child feeling ashamed of the true self's unrewarded striving (Wells & Jones, 2000). The child develops caretaking as a primary source of identity, so that *not* caretaking perversely becomes a *denial of self*. The parentification style of parenting one's parent typically leads to overprotectiveness, while the parentification style of parenting one's siblings typically leads to submissiveness and dependence (Marx, 1999).

11 (page 149) Recent research results estimate that, compared with those who had not experienced multiple traumas at birth, men who had experienced such trauma run an almost 5 times greater risk for violent suicide, and women run a slightly higher risk (Jacobson & Bygdeman, 1998).

Feldmar (1979) studied a number of adolescent patients with a history of more than five suicide attempts each, always at the same time of year. He eventually determined that the suicide dates of four patients corresponded to the month in which their mothers had tried to abort them. The adolescents had no *conscious* knowledge of the abortion attempts that they were *unconsciously* acting out. Feldmar discovered that they had even used a method of suicide similar to the method of the abortion, for example, chemicals or instruments. After discovering that their suicide attempts were seasonal intrusions of prenatal memory, the patients were free of the suicidal compulsion. They never attempted suicide again, even when their 'anniversaries' returned.

12 (page 153) The term *corrective emotional experience* was first used by psychoanalyst Franz Alexander (1946). He stated that in all forms of psychotherapy "the basic therapeutic principle is the same: to reexpose the patient, under more favorable circumstances, to emotional situations which he could not handle in the past. The patient, in order to be helped, must undergo a corrective emotional experience suitable to repair the traumatic influence of previous experiences. ... Re-experiencing the old, unsettled conflict *but with a new ending* is the secret of every penetrating therapeutic result." The actual experience of a new solution convinces the individual

that a new solution is possible, provides an incentive for him to give up the old neurotic patterns, and creates a new prototype for what can replace the old. Then, through repetition, these corrected reactions gradually become automatic; the ego accepts the new behavior patterns and integrates them into the total personality.

[13] (page 154) The concept of children generalizing their experience into early conclusions about themselves and the world is widely held. For example, Barbara Findeisen describes this situation (Mendizza): "Memories of early trauma are there, underneath the surface. They're there in our dreams, attitudes, even in our vocabulary. People unconsciously walk around in them all day but are not aware of where they come from. Many times after a birth regression clients say, 'I live this pattern every day. It never occurred to me that it might start that early'."

In Heart-Centered therapies we have used the term *early conclusions* to denote the basic deeply embedded (mistaken) beliefs about self and the world from the earliest experiences, which then are carried forward in time as templates for how one sees the world and functions in it. We have traced them back very early in life, to birth, to the womb, and even to the process of conception.

If not dissipated through corrective experience, these deeply embedded prototypes for life will exert profound influence, as we have seen, over the individual's lifespan. Repatterning or re-framing provides an opportunity for the individual to release any dysfunctional beliefs remaining from early experience, and to replace them with healthier, more functional patterns.

In the field of attachment theory, these generalized conclusions are called *internal working models* (see endnote 8, page 170).

Berne, in *Games People Play*, talks about the defensive "solution" that a child develops as a way to deal with the threat of a recurrence of trauma as a *decision*. These decisions become habitual, in what Berne calls the person's *script, life position* or *life plan*. Regarding therapy, Berne stated that anything that is learned can be unlearned; anything that is decided can be redecided.

Woollams (1977, p. 359), in discussing these early life *script decisions*, says that the "awareness of the decisions we made as children, which resulted in our life plans or scripts, leads to the notion that we therefore can make new decisions – redecisions – *now* about how we are going to live."

We have found that the hypnotic age regression provides an ideal method of accessing the original child ego state that made those decisions and developed the life script, and can most effectively change them to create new healthier life *script decisions* (see endnote 6, page 169).

References

Abramson, L., Seligman, M., & Teasdale, J. (1978). Learned helplessness in humans: Critique and reformulation. *Journal of Abnormal Psychology*, 87, 49-74.

Alexander, F., French, T. M. *et al.* (1946). *Psychoanalytic Therapy: Principles and Application.* New York: Ronald Press.

Berne, E. (1964). *Games People Play.* New York: Ballantine Books.

Biringen, Z., Robinson, J. L., & Emde, R. N. (1994). Maternal sensitivity in the second year of life: Gender-based relations in the dyadic balance of control. *American Journal of Orthopsychiatry*, 64, 78-90.

Bowlby, J. (1969/1982). *Attachment and Loss: Vol. 1. Attachment.* New York: Basic Books.

Bowlby, J. (1980). *Attachment and Loss: Vol. 3. Loss: Sadness and Depression.* New York: Basic Books.

Bradshaw, J. (1988). *Healing the Shame that Binds You.* Deerfield Beach, FL: Health Communications.

de Groot, J. M., & Rodin, G. (1994). Eating disorders, female psychology, and the self. *Journal of the American Academy of Psychoanalysis*, 22(2), 299-317.

Feldmar, A. (1979). The embryology of consciousness: What is a normal pregnancy? In D. Mall & W. Watts (Eds.), *The Psychological Aspects of Abortion*, 15-24. University Publications of America.

Holloway, W. H. (1977). Transactional analysis: An integrative approach. In G. Barnes, (Ed.), *Transactional Analysis after Eric Berne*, 169-221. New York: Harper's College Press.

Jacobson, B., & Bygdeman, M. (1998). Birth trauma linked to violent suicide. *British Medical Journal*, 317, 1346-1349.

Karpman, S. (April 1968). *Transactional Analysis Bulletin, 7*, no. 26.

Maddi, S., & Kobasa, S. (1984). *The Hardy Executive: Health Under Stress.* Homewood, IL: Dow Jones-Irwin.

Marx, E. L. (1999). The relationship of parentification and adult adaptation in female social work graduate students (women students). *Dissertation Abstracts International: Section A: Humanities and Social Sciences*, 59(10-A), 3753.

Mendizza, M. *Lifelong Patterns: Fear or Wholeness?* Michael Mendizza Interviews Barbara Findeisen. Available online at http://www.birthpsychology.com/lifebefore/early6.html.

Norwood, R. (1985). *Women Who Love Too Much: When You Keep Wishing and Hoping He'll Change.* Los Angeles: Jeremy P. Tarcher.

Pound, A. (1982). Attachment and maternal depression. In C. M. Parkes & J. Stevenson-Hinde (Eds.), *The Place of Attachment in Human Behavior*, 118-130. New York: Basic Books.

Robinson, J. L., & Biringen, Z. (1995). Gender and emerging autonomy in development. *Psychoanalytic Inquiry*.

Robinson, J. L., Little, C., & Biringen, Z. (1993). Emotional communication in mother-toddler relationships: Evidence for early gender differentiation. *Merrill-Palmer Quarterly*, 39, 496-517.

Root, M. P. P. (1992). Reconstructing the impact of trauma on personality. In S. Brown & M. Ballou (Eds.), *Personality and Psychopathology*, 229-265. New York: Guilford.

Rossi, E. L., & Cheek, D. (1988). *Mind-Body Therapy: Ideodynamic Healing in Hypnosis.* New York: W. W. Norton.

Ruppert, E., & Ziff, J. (July 1994). The mind, body, and soul of violence. *Transactional Analysis Journal*, 24(3), 161-177.

Watkins, J. G., & Watkins, H. H. (1982). Ego-state therapy. In L. E. Abt & I. R. Stuart (Eds.), *The Newer Therapies: A Sourcebook*, 136-155. New York: Van Nostrand Reinhold.

Wells, M., & Jones, R. (2000). Childhood parentification and shame-proneness: A preliminary study. *American Journal of Family Therapy*, 28(1), 19-27.

Winnicott, D. (1960). Ego distortion in terms of true and false self. In *The Maturational Processes and the Facilitating Environment.* New York: International University Press.

Woollams, S. J. (1977). From 21 to 43. In G. Barnes, (Ed.), *Transactional Analysis after Eric Berne*, 351-379. New York: Harper's College Press.

Zahn-Waxler, C., & Radke-Yarrow, M. (1990). The origins of empathic concern. *Motivation and Emotion*, 14, 107-130.

Zimberoff, D., & Hartman, D. (1998). Insidious trauma caused by prenatal gender prejudice. *Journal of Prenatal and Perinatal Psychology and Health*, 13(1), 45-51.

Index

Index

Interested in finding a Heart-Centered therapist in your area?
Please contact The Wellness Institute at 425-391-9716 or 800-326-4418.
Or use the online Directory of certified Heart-Centered therapists.

www.heartcenteredtherapies.org

Heart-Centered Therapies

Search for Therapists

Select a country:
Select from list ▼

Or if USA, select a state:
Select from list ▼

SEARCH   RESET

Heart-Centered Therapies Association
3716 - 274th Avenue SE
Issaquah, WA 98029 USA
Phone: 1-800-914-8348

If you are a professional interested in becoming trained and certified in Heart-Centered Hypnotherapy, contact The Wellness Institute at 425-391-9716 or 800-326-4418. Or find further information online.

www.wellness-institute.org

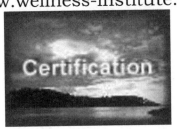
Certification

The Wellness Institute
3716 274th Avenue SE, Issaquah, WA 98029, USA. Telephone: 425-391-9716

Journal of Heart-Centered Therapies

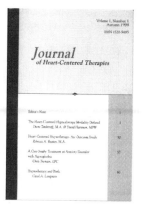

The *Journal of Heart-Centered Therapies* is published twice each year and is available by subscription. A full set of back issues are provided to new subscribers. The *Journal* is a peer-reviewed publication of the research findings and clinical experience of practitioners of Heart-Centered therapies. It is intended to provide a forum for the many clinicians around the world who are utilizing Heart-Centered therapies in their healing work.

Some articles from previous issues of the *Journal*:

* Heart-Centered Therapies and the Christian Spiritual Path
* A Buddhist Perspective in Heart-Centered Therapies
* The Existential Approach in Heart-Centered Therapies
* Ego States in Heart-Centered Therapies
* Gestalt Therapy and Heart-Centered Therapies
* Hypnotic Trance in Heart-Centered Therapies
* Transpersonal Psychology in Heart-Centered Therapies
* Memory Access to our Earliest Influences
* Attachment, Detachment, Nonattachment: Achieving Synthesis
* Four Primary Existential Themes in Heart-Centered Therapies
* Existential Issues in Heart-Centered therapies: A Developmental Approach
* The Ego in Heart-Centered Therapies:
* Breathwork: Exploring the Frontier of 'Being' and 'Doing'
* Heart-Centered Energetic Psychodrama
* Personal Transformation with Heart-Centered Therapies
* The Heart-Centered Hypnotherapy Modality Defined

The Heart-Centered Therapies Association

3716 274th Avenue SE, Issaquah, WA 98029, USA. Telephone: 425-391-9716

Materials available from Diane Zimberoff
online at http://www.wellness-institute.org

On these pages are listed some of the CDs and audiotapes that you may find helpful in your personal search for healing.

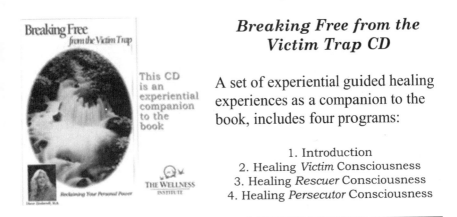

Breaking Free from the Victim Trap CD

A set of experiential guided healing experiences as a companion to the book, includes four programs:

1. Introduction
2. Healing *Victim* Consciousness
3. Healing *Rescuer* Consciousness
4. Healing *Persecutor* Consciousness

Self-help CDs and Audiotapes from Diane:

1. Codependency
2. Extinguishing Unwanted Behaviors
3. Healing and meditation
4. Prosperity
5. Sales Improvement *(set of 2)*
6. Self-esteem and Parenting *(set of 2)*
7. Self-hypnosis Program *(set of 2)*
8. Strengthening the Immune System
9. Success Program *(set of 2)*
10. Visualization & Eliminating Stress
11. Women and Success
12. Women Who Love Too Much

The Wellness Institute
3716 274th Avenue SE, Issaquah, WA 98029, USA. Telephone: 425-391-9716

Personal Transformation Meditation: The Chakras

A two-CD set with five meditations:

1. Introduction To Meditation
2. Activating Lower Chakras
3. Activating Higher Chakras
4. Soul Retrieval Meditation
5. Mind - Body - Spirit Healing

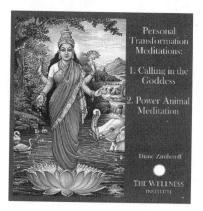

Personal Transformation Meditations

One
CALLING IN THE GODDESS
Inviting the Goddess in
to open each Chakra

Two
POWER ANIMAL MEDITATION
Discovering the Power Animal
in each Chakra and
finding its individual message

You will find these and other products that Diane has created to enhance your personal growth at the online store

http://www.wellness-institute.org/

The Wellness Institute
3716 274th Avenue SE, Issaquah, WA 98029, USA. Telephone: 425-391-9716

TWO PROGRAMS FROM THE WELLNESS INSTITUTE
Available nationally through a network of affiliated providers
1-800-326-4418

Stop Smoking Program

Follow this step-by-step program, which includes an activity
workbook and audiotapes for reinforcement. You will be a
permanent non-smoker by the end of four weeks.

TRIM-LIFE
Weight Release Program

"Diets Don't Work - The Power of your Mind Does"

Discover the *emotional reasons* for your unhealthy eating
patterns, and you will release them *once and for all*!